MY NAME IS KATE AND I JUST KILLED MY BABY

by Duane L. Ostler

TABLE OF CONTENTS
(KATE'S JOURNAL ENTRIES)

April 16 1
April 17 3
April 19 10
April 20 20
April 22 29
April 24 38
April 25 40
April 26 45
April 28 56
April 29 62
April 30 69
May 1 77
May 4 88
May 12 93
May 14 104
May 17 112
May 20 122
May 21 127
May 23 133
May 24 141
May 25 151
May 28 159
May 31 165
Other books by the author 176

This book is dedicated to:
the unborn,
who have no choice.

APRIL 16

My name is Katherine Anderson. I go by Kate. I am 18 years old, and live on the outskirts of Pittsburgh, Pennsylvania in a little place called Cranberry Township. My Dad is an accountant at a nearby shoe factory. His name is Paul. My mother is a housewife, and her name is Carol. She used to work as a beautician, but lately she's been sick a lot.

I like pizza and ice cream, and going on dates and funny movies. I used to have my own car, but it's in the shop right now. I have a pet cat named 'Oscar' who is absolutely adorable. He is a big, grey Maine coon, and likes to get into things he shouldn't and wake people up in the middle of the night. I love him lots, but unfortunately he's lost right now. I hope he comes back soon.

I've gotten good grades in school most of my life, and my Dad and Mom always just assumed I would go to college. I assumed it too until recently. But lately school has become a lot harder, and I'm not sure anymore what I'm going to do with my life.

I like to swim, and to text on my cell phone, and in high school for awhile I was on the girl's drill team. I like skiing in the winter, and I used to love curling up with a good book in front of a fire afterward. I enjoy cooking and picking out clothes, and wearing new shoes. I guess you could say I'm a pretty typical girl in most respects.

Oh, there's one more thing you should know about me. I just killed my baby.

APRIL 17

You're probably wondering why I ended so abruptly above. After all, to end such a normal description of a normal-sounding person with something so shocking just doesn't add up. Well, if you had a magic window and could look through it and see the way my life has gone for the last while, you wouldn't wonder. It would all be plain to you. I couldn't keep writing after I said I'd killed my baby. I just couldn't. The images of Jonathon were haunting me too much, and the tears started to come again, and it's awful hard to write very legibly when you can't see through your tears.

My therapist told me I should write this, and that's the only reason I'm doing it. He told me to write the whole story from the beginning, even though it started a year ago. That's when I killed my baby. So I suppose what I said above isn't strictly correct. I didn't 'just' kill my baby. But every day when I first wake up it seems like I just did, when it all comes back to me.

My therapist told me it would help somehow to write in this journal, to sort through my feelings. It hasn't helped so far. When I looked back today and read what I wrote above, I just wanted to take this journal and throw it as far out into the river as I could.

But my therapist wouldn't like that. He made me promise to show it to him, and prove that I've been writing. So I overcame the urge to throw it in the river, and decided to write in it instead.

I suppose the only way any of this is going to make sense is to go back to the beginning, and tell my story in the way it happened just like my therapist said. He would like that. He's always saying silly things like, "No one can understand themselves until they understand their beginnings." Then he goes on and on about how the fourth of July is all about remembering our nation's beginnings, and so are high school reunions and memorial parks and birthdays and cemeteries and museums. He says if we suddenly didn't have all those things anymore, we'd be confused, not knowing who we are, because our beginnings would be missing.

But of course I don't believe him. If I could somehow forget the beginnings of my story I KNOW I'd be a lot happier. I wish I could forget. Oh, how I wish that.

But I'm getting off on a tangent, which is what Mom always used to say I shouldn't do, at least before she got sick. "Don't get off on a tangent, Kate--when you start a job, stay with it and get it done." I can hear her voice in my mind, and the memory makes me smile. I wish she would say it again. But lately she hasn't been saying much of anything. And she's not as organized as she used to be. The house was never messy like it is now, and the clothes were never piled up, and the dishes were always washed. Mom never got off on tangents. That is, until recently, and I'm the cause of that.

But again, I'm off on a tangent. Mom may not be avoiding tangents anymore, but I'm going to. I'm going to try to do everything she ever told me to do. Maybe that way I can make it up to her.

It all started when I found out I was pregnant. That was about a year ago. Bob and I had been seeing each other for quite awhile. We knew we shouldn't have gotten that physically involved, and I felt horribly bad about it afterward, but it happened. We didn't do it again, I'm glad to say, even though Bob wanted to. I didn't let him. Now, a little more than a month had passed since we'd had our big night, and even though I'd had a nagging worry I might be pregnant, I'd managed to avoid thinking about it. How could I be pregnant from just one time? But lately the nagging feeling had gotten stronger and my clothes had started shrinking and my body hadn't been acting according to its normal clock, so I figured I'd better take the test. When I did, it came out positive.

Bob was not happy. "This can't be happening!" he kept saying over and over when I told him that night. He ran a shaking hand through his hair and stared at me with a crazed look in his eyes. Then he started to rant and rave about how we should have done things differently. After that he started to blame me for not doing things differently, to prevent this from happening. But I hardly heard him. I was still too much in a daze from finding out earlier that day that the test was positive.

A baby. I was going to have a baby. Me. ME! A little life was starting inside me, and soon it would come out and be mine. I just couldn't get over it.

I also didn't know what to think about it. Part of me felt just like Bob, and was horrified and just wanted it to all go away. But another part of me was curious and almost happy, as if I'd always wanted a little one like Jonathon to come into my life.

Jonathon was his name from the very beginning. I always knew that he would be a boy, and that would be his name. What I'm less certain about is why. Maybe it's because of my Uncle Jonathon who was in the navy until he was killed in a freak accident at sea. Or maybe it's because in fifth grade when my friend Clarice and I used to make up names we'd give to our babies someday, she always laughed and chided me whenever I mentioned Jonathon. Somehow, that made it a helpless name to be defended, just like little Jonathon was helpless now, and needed to be defended.

Or maybe it's just because I've always liked words with three syllables. Like 'wonderful,' or 'tapestry' or 'anchoves.' Somehow three syllable words just roll naturally off your tongue, and have a wonderful feel to them. I used to try and make up whole sentences made just of three syllable words. The best I could ever do was 'Jonathon's wonderful ancestry underwent difficult temptations.' I know that doesn't make much sense, but it did to me when I was in fifth grade.

So now that I was pregnant, I just knew this baby was a boy and his name was Jonathon. And listening to Bob rant and rave about what a big problem Jonathon was, I suddenly felt like I was back in fifth grade defending his name from Clarice's teasing.

"Jonathon is not a problem!" I said firmly, looking Bob in the eye. "He's a baby. And nothing you say will change that."

Bob looked at me as if broccoli had just sprouted out of my nose. "Jonathon!" he roared. "You've given it a name? Are you crazy? Giving it a name just makes it worse! You can't have this baby!"

I blinked in surprise. "Why?" I blurted without thinking.

Bob started to wave his hands wildly, and for a minute I wondered if he was going to punch me. "Because you're not supposed to be pregnant!" he screamed. "Do you know what my parents will say when they find out? Do you know what they will DO?" His voice had risen to a screech that sounded almost like a little girl. Then he started waving his finger in my face. "And what about your parents? What will they say? Your Mom will have a cow, for Pete's sake! And I can just imagine how your Dad will blow his top!"

He was right, of course. I'd known that from the instant the test came back positive. So far I'd managed to shut it out of my mind. But somehow his saying it made it seem real for the first time, as if I'd just barely recognized how badly they would react to the news.

"But how can I NOT have this baby?" I said stupidly. "You can't turn things like this on and off like a faucet."

"Yes you can," said Bob firmly, taking me by the shoulders and looking me in the eye. His intensity startled me. "Abortion. That's the answer. That's what you have to do. I'll pay for it. I'm sure I've got enough money saved up."

The word spat at me like an angry bee. "Abortion!" I blurted. "I can't do that!"

"Why not?" countered Bob. "You're old enough--you just turned 18! You don't need your parent's permission. It's a simple procedure, and there's a clinic down the hill in Pittsburgh. And this way, no one will ever know."

I stared at Bob, speechless. Finally I said, "There's got to be another way. We could always get married."

"Are you nuts?" he cried, waving his hands wildly again. "You know I was held back a year, so I'm still only a junior in high school! Unlike you, I won't graduate for over a year! My part time job sacking groceries can't support us! Get real, will you?"

I continued to stare at him, my mind still resisting the idea of an abortion. "Then why not just let it be born and give it up for adoption?" I asked.

"Yeah, right!" he cried, rolling his eyes. "Then the whole world will know! Your Dad might even kick you out! You know how strict he is! Where would you go then? You don't have money to support yourself, and like I said, neither do I!"

Seeing me about to protest further, he said again, but more firmly this time, "Just do it! Have an abortion. You HAVE to do it--you have no choice. And no one will ever know."

My mouth snapped shut, and I didn't say anything. My mind was in a blur, and it felt like there was a buzzing in my head that wouldn't stop. My emotions were a huge ocean wave, breaking on the rocks of a sea shore. But in the midst of it all, one simple thought stood out that could not be denied.

I would know.

APRIL 19

My therapist is a liar. A big, fat liar. Writing in this stupid journal has not helped at all. All it's done is bring back all the memories and all the pain and all the heartache I went through before. How can that be helpful? That's like telling someone who just recovered from a broken leg to go out and break it again.

So why am I writing in here once more, if it's such a painful waste? Beats me. I can't figure it out. It makes no more sense than liking three syllable words. But here I am doing it again, regardless of anything. I must be nuts.

Which is probably a fair assessment. Because I was just nutty enough to start taking seriously what Bob said about having an abortion. After all, I just KNEW that if my parents found out, it would break their hearts. The whole rest of our date that night Bob kept talking about it. After I left him, all I could think about was having an abortion. And when I went to bed that night I just lay there tossing and turning, with thoughts of an abortion still running through my mind. Oscar kept brushing up against me with his furry head, but I pushed him away. Bob's intense face kept leering at me out of the dark, mumbling the words "Have an abortion!" "Have an abortion!" "Have an abortion!"

Finally I got up and went to see if there was any leftover pizza in the fridge. Not that I was hungry or anything, since my stomach felt tied up in knots. I mainly needed something to do. I found some pizza and tried to keep the microwave quiet while I cooked it, but I guess I wasn't successful. I'd only taken one tiny bite when Mom showed up in the kitchen.

"Is anything wrong, Kate?" she asked, her eyes bleary from having just woken up. She always was a light sleeper.

"No, nothing at all," I said as pleasantly as I could at 2:00 am, with the question of an abortion weighing on my mind like an anvil.

Mom was always pretty perceptive, and didn't believe a word of it. She gave me a shrewd look, then said, "You had a fight with Bob. Is that it?"

"Yes," I jibbered, feeling an unaccountable wave of relief that she didn't know the real reason. "We did sort of have a fight ..."

"Well, don't let it get you down," said Mom, smiling and coming over to give me a little hug. "Your father and I used to have little fights all the time when we were dating, about all sorts of things. We still do, in fact. But that doesn't mean he doesn't care for you. Things will sort themselves out. You'll feel a lot better when the sun comes up in the morning."

That's another one of Mom's favorite sayings. Things will always be better when the sun comes up in the morning. I just wish it were true, both for her and for me. She never repeats this saying anymore, and these days she doesn't usually look like she feels any better when the sun comes up. Neither do I. But in the kitchen that night, she seemed to believe it. And silly me, I did too.

"Sure, Mom," I agreed with a slight smile. "It's nothing. It'll blow over. It's no big deal." I gave her a little hug, then put my pizza down since I really wasn't hungry. "I think I'll go back to bed now." Then I wandered down the hall, wondering to myself whether being pregnant and having an abortion was a big deal or not. After all, lots of women had abortions. It didn't seem to bother them, so why should it bother me? And it was perfectly legal, so it must be ok. Those smart men in government wouldn't let it be legal if there was anything wrong with it, would they?

But I didn't sleep any better than I had before. Seeing me so restless, Oscar came over again and tried to pry his furry head under my arm. I pushed him away, after which he walked away in disgust with his tail in the air, like offended cats do.

By morning I was a basket case. I needed to talk to someone. I just couldn't keep all this bottled up inside. Bob was no help, and I couldn't tell Mom or Dad. There was obviously only one person to turn to.

Clarice. My childhood friend, who was still my closest advisor even after all these years. I tried to text her the minute I got up, but there was no response. Silly me. I knew she never looked at her texts this early. Finally I ducked out of the house, giving Mom some excuse about how I wanted to catch Clarice before school and I'd drive us both there. Then I raced over to her house in my car.

"Oh, hello Kate!" said Clarice's Mom at the door, giving me a big smile. I found myself wondering what there was to smile about. "Clarice is upstairs getting ready for school." Then she walked away, since she was used to me coming over and invading their house. I did it all the time.

"I've got to talk to you," I said as I came into Clarice's bathroom where she was doing her hair. She just frowned at me. Her opinion of hair was very intense, as if it needed all of her concentration. Normally if I came in and found her doing her hair, I knew better than to barge around like a rat in a dollhouse, and just remained silent until she was done.

But today I couldn't wait. Not after the horrible night I'd had. And unlike my normal personality, I decided the blunt approach might be the best way to overcome her fixation with hair. I only hoped I didn't shock her so much she burned her hand on her curling iron.

"I'm pregnant," I said boldly, my voice suddenly sounding strange and far away as if even my own mouth could not believe what it was saying. "And Bob wants me to have an abortion."

Clarice dropped her curling iron with a clatter, her eyes opening big as garbage can lids. "You're kidding!" she gasped, her face turning white. My face had turned pretty white too, and I suddenly felt lightheaded at having blurted something so unthinkable without any preliminary. I took a quick step over to her bed and sat down.

She knew I wasn't kidding by the look on my face. She and I kidded each other a lot, so perhaps it wasn't surprising she would wonder--

especially when I came in and blurted it out like that. But she could tell this was for real. She just stared at me as she went over and sat down next to me on the bed. "I can't believe it!"

I was surprised to see that my hands were shaking. "Neither can I," I answered in a rather husky voice.

"Have you told you parents?" she asked.

"Are you kidding?" I barked. "You know how they are! All that stuff at church about how you're not supposed to do this sort of thing. They think holding hands is a sin! It took my Dad three months before he stopped glaring at Bob every time he came to take me out. How could I tell them?"

"My goodness!" was all Clarice could say.

"Hey, don't pretend like this is all that shocking," I retorted. "I've seen the way you and Tom carry on when you're on dates. I know Bob and I did wrong by getting so involved, and we'll have to account for it to God someday. And believe me, the way I feel now I have no intention of ever giving him more than a good night kiss from now on! But I can't change my condition. I can't go back in time and undo it."

"My goodness," said Clarice again, raising a hand to smooth her hair, and messing it up worse in the process. "I just can't believe it!"

"Will you stop saying that?" I said through gritted teeth. "You don't know how bad of a night I've had! Bob kept pushing me to get an abortion. It was all he could talk about last night. He practically made me promise I would. He kept saying I have no choice, that I HAVE to do it. But I just don't know if I feel right about it. Somehow it seems wrong, you know what I mean?" I stood up suddenly and paced over to the window.

"Oh, Kate," said Clarice, coming over to stand next to me. "This is awful!"

"Tell me about it," I said gruffly. She put her hand on my shoulder, and suddenly to my surprise tears started to come. And before I knew it I broke down and balled like a stupid little two-year-old. Clarice hadn't seen me cry like that since kindergarten.

I guess it sort of got to her too, since she suddenly started balling as well. The two of us were a sight, both blubbering like walruses with head colds. We went on like that for quite awhile, too. Most normal parents would have been up yelling at their daughter that she was going to be late for school. But we both knew Clarice's Mom had gone to work already, leaving her to get to school on her own. And we both knew today was a day that we'd be late to class.

"Oh, Kate," said Clarice in a blubbery voice when we finally started getting hold of ourselves. "This is awful! Just awful!"

"You said that already," I replied, trying weakly to grin at her.

"No, you don't understand," she said, looking at me through tear-streaked eyes. "You see, a few weeks ago Tom and I kind of ... well we shouldn't have, and I feel real bad about it and would never do it again, but--"

"No!" I blurted. "Don't tell me--"

"I don't know yet," answered Clarice. "I've been testing every day since, and so far it hasn't come back positive. But it still could. And

Tom's been saying the same as Bob, that if it does happen, I should have an abortion."

Now it was my turn. "Oh, Clarice!" I said, staring at her with wide eyes. "This is awful!"

She suddenly grinned, her chin trembling. "Isn't it, though? Now I understand why my Dad never liked Tom and was always so strict about when he brought me home after dates. He was trying to prevent something like this. Oh, I wish I hadn't done it! I feel so terrible! If only I'd known it would make me feel like this! And trying to hide it makes it worse, since I have to hide if from Mom and Dad and even you ..."

"Hey," I said, giving her a friendly pat on the arm. "You don't have to hide it from me anymore. I'm in the same boat, remember? And I feel just as bad about having done it as you do. But now I'm pregnant and I have to make a decision. And I need your advice."

Clarice just looked at me, her eyes welling up with water as if the dam was about to burst again. "An abortion," she said in a soft voice, but in a way that made it sound ugly. "I know exactly how you feel, Kate. I've been wondering the same thing. And Tom's been telling me every day that I HAVE to do it if I test positive, that I don't have any choice--"

"Why do he and Bob keep saying that?" I practically yelled. "If I don't have a choice, how come I I have an awful choice to make? And if I don't have a choice, how come they're always saying in the news that abortion is a woman's choice? It IS a choice! And this choice involves more than just me! It involves--"

"Don't say it!" screeched Clarice. Now her chin was wobbling and trembling for all it was worth. "I've been looking into it, and it's not what you think it is. It's just a little lump of cells. Just like cancer, or a wart. It's not a baby yet. Abortion isn't like killing it. It's just removing un unwanted growth, that's all."

I stared at Clarice, dumfounded. Never had I thought I would hear such words coming out of her mouth. She was always the outspoken one on issues, that couldn't keep her mouth shut. I on the other hand usually kept quiet and let others have their opinions. We'd never talked about abortion before, but I had never imagined that she would be in favor of it.

"After all," she continued in a stilted voice, as if she was trying to convince herself more than me, "the Supreme Court has said a woman has the choice of what to do with her body. And if she wants a growth removed, she can do it, no questions asked. It's her right. And there's nothing wrong with it!"

"But the baby--" I started to say.

"It's not a baby!" she cried, waving her hands around wildly. "It's just a thing! A cell growth gone mad!" Trying to compose herself, she ran a shaking hand through her hair, messing it up even more. "Look at it this way," she said in what was an attempt at a calmer voice. "There are lots of contraceptives on the market today. That's all abortion is--a prevention of pregnancy. If there's no sin in using contraceptives, surely there's no sin in an abortion. It's exactly the same thing!"

"But a contraceptive prevents life from even getting started," I countered. "That's way different. If it doesn't get started, it doesn't get started. Abortion on the other hand deals with it after it's started, when it could keep going and--"

"It's not a life!" cried Clarice shrilly, trying to drown me out. "It's just a blob of flesh that has to be removed! That's what you have to keep constantly in mind. It's not a life! It's not! It's just a blob of cells, like cancer!"

There was silence in her room for a moment. A very awkward silence. We just looked at each other, knowing that this was a defining moment not only in our friendship, but in our lives. The minutes ticked by. But I knew I had to voice the question that, to me, made all the difference. After all, Clarice was the most tender hearted of all the people I knew. If she believed abortion was a harmless procedure, then maybe it was acceptable after all.

"Do you really believe that?" I asked softly at last. "That it's not a real life yet, that it's just a blob of cells, that abortion is no different than using a contraceptive? Because if you're wrong, if it really IS a life, if there really is a little person named Jonathon--"

"Kate!" said Clarice firmly, gripping my arm so tightly it was sure to leave a mark. "Don't give it a name! Trust me! It's not a life yet! It's just a blob of cells. You're not doing anything wrong by having it removed. And after you've had it taken out, you can go back to exactly the way life was before ..."

I just stared at her without saying a word. I had my answer. I finally knew what I had to do. And Clarice seemed so certain, surely she was right. How could it be wrong after all to merely remove a few cells?

Yet in spite of it all, my eyes were starting to feel like they would play 'water fountain' again in a minute. I was engulfed by a profound sense of sadness, as if I were a distant observer who had just witnessed a horrible accident. It was a sadness that gripped my heart with tender firmness, not letting go no matter how hard I tried to shake it.

"Right," I said at last. "It's just a blob of cells to be removed. And after the abortion's over, my life will go back to just the way it was before. Just the same. No different ..."

But what my heart knew and didn't say was that it would be a life without Jonathon.

APRIL 20

I hate this stinking journal. I hate it so bad I want to rip it to shreds or flush it down the toilet, or put tomato sauce on it and put it in the microwave until it explodes. Every time I come back to it my eyes fixate and I read the whole stupid thing over again, and then I relive all the horror I felt before. This journal is like a dozen massive paper cuts that never go away.

So why haven't I destroyed it yet? What insanity has not only made me keep it, but start writing in it again? My lousy therapist, that's what. My appointment with him is tomorrow, and he's going to ask if I've finished writing my full story yet, from the beginning. Well, obviously I haven't. It's been a year since my abortion, and I've only written about the first few days before the abortion even happened. Stupid therapist. I'm going to grit my teeth and take it in to show him that I've been writing in it, even though I haven't finished. And right after the appointment I'm going to take it out and throw it down the nearest sewer outlet on the street I see.

So, here I go again. I'm writing in this wretched thing when I should be doing anything else. I know that what comes next in my story is the most horrid part of all, and once I write it, if I ever read it later it will destroy me. That's why I have to destroy it tomorrow by throwing it down the sewer. Then I'll never have to read it again. I'll just tell my therapist I lost it or something. Or maybe that it was put in the wash by mistake.

And so, to continue my story, the next day I made an appointment over the phone at the abortion clinic in Pittsburgh. They said I could come down that very day, to have my pregnancy confirmed, fill out some forms and make the necessary appointments. Feeling like a zombie, I drove down to the clinic. When I got there I was surprised to see it looked like any typical medical building, just like many I've seen dozens of times while driving down the road. Funny, I guess I'd expected to see a big neon sign over it screaming out 'Abortions Happen Here!' Or maybe I thought I'd see some anti-abortion people yelling and chanting slogans in front of the door, and throwing tomatoes at the people who went inside. But there weren't any.

I sat in my car for a full ten minutes before I could build up the courage to go in. It took almost another five minutes before I made it to the door, the way I shuffled along. My heart just wasn't in it. I'd done all the convincing I was capable of and kept telling myself there was no choice, that I had to do this, that it was just a blob of flesh like a wart being removed, and that there was nothing to get so upset about. But my heart kept pounding like crazy in my chest even though I was barely walking along at a snail's pace.

The hardest thing I ever did was to push that door open. I wish now it had been too hard for me, that I hadn't been able to get it open. Then my story would be different, and Jonathon would still be part of it.

But stupid me, I pushed the door open at last and staggered inside. A dozen people looked up at me as I walked in, making me feel unaccountably ashamed to even be there. But I quickly noticed most of them were young girls like me. I was appalled to see that two of the girls had an older woman with them--who apparently was their mother! These girls were probably under 18, and needed a parent's consent. The idea of my mother ever coming with me into a place like this was unthinkable. What mother would do such a thing? Most of the girls had dead eyes, which is probably how my eyes looked too. It was plain none of us wanted to be here, or to be faced with what we were faced with. Yet the truth was, every one of us had made choices with our boyfriends that put us here--choices that could have been made differently. We weren't here by accident.

"Can I help you?" asked the receptionist as I came up to the front desk.

"I ... I ..." I stammered, my voice cracking. I tried again, in a whisper so as not to be heard even though everyone knew why I had come. "I need to have a ..."

"Certainly," said the receptionist, mercifully cutting me off. Apparently she had witnessed this scene many times before. "Do you have an appointment?" she asked. I confirmed that I did. She did some quick checking, then said, "You're in luck. You can go straight in. You just need to have a simple test to verify the pregnancy, and to determine the gestational age. I'll have you fill out your forms once you come out."

I walked like a zombie through the door she pointed out. The test was quickly performed by a guy named Doctor Peterson, and confirmed my pregnancy as I knew it would. Dr. Peterson seemed nice enough, and said he would likely be the one to perform the abortion.

When I came back out the receptionist handed me a clipboard. "Here are some forms to fill out," she said. "Please make sure to fill out the medical release on page two. And please read this notice, regarding abortions under Pennsylvania law. By law you're required to receive counseling from a physician 24 hours before the procedure is performed."

"Really?" I said, letting out a huge breath of relief. That could be my excuse! The counseling would probably cost extra money for Bob and take extra time, and naturally it would be too much of an imposition ...

"The counseling can be provided here or over the phone, and is part of our total cost," said the receptionist. "Since you already met with Doctor Peterson who usually provides the counseling, he will probably do it for you over the phone. Do you have a cell phone? Make sure you list the number on that form, and he will call you 24 hours before your appointment. Once you bring back those papers I'll take a look at our schedule and see when it can be done."

"Will it be a long time before you can do it?" I asked, almost in hope. If it would be a whole month before it could happen, that could be an escape as well.

She must have thought I wanted it done fast. "We can usually do it in two to three days," she replied with a kindly smile, making my heart sink. "Are you in a hurry?"

"No," I gushed. "I was just curious." I took the clipboard and stumbled over to a chair where I started to fill out the papers. I noticed my hands were shaking as I did so.

"Is this your first, dearie?" asked a voice suddenly. Startled, I looked up to see a middle-aged woman smiling at me from two seats over.

"Yes," I said uncertainly.

"Don't worry about it, honey," she said gently. "I've had two done here. They're very good. You don't feel a thing."

"That's not what I'm worried about," I blurted before I could stop myself.

She smiled knowingly, instantly understanding what I meant. "Don't worry about that either," she said reassuringly. "This is your right. No one can force you to stay pregnant if you don't want to be. It's your body, not anybody else's. No one will be hurt by this. No one."

No one will be hurt? What about Jonathon? Wasn't he somebody, and wouldn't he be hurt? As if the woman could read my mind (and had been talking to my friend Clarice) she said, "Don't worry about it. It's not a life yet. It's just a blob of cells, nothing more. It won't feel anything. I've had two, dearie, so I know." She suddenly blinked rapidly for some reason, making me notice that she seemed to be wearing a lot of mascara.

I shook my head dumbly, then bent to the task of filling out the forms. They were not overly complicated, and merely asked the usual questions about my health history and whether I was on any medications. One form asked my age and the date of my last period and the estimated date of conception. It also asked the best time for the physician to call me, which I naturally put during the school day rather than the evening. Imagine getting such a call at home! Obviously I would skip class at the time of the call.

I found myself shivering as I filled it out, and I'm afraid some of my responses were not very legible I wrote so fast. I suddenly had an overpowering urge just to get out of there, and especially away from the "Dearie" woman who kept looking at me. I finished the form with a flourish and took it back quickly to the receptionist. She smiled at me as she took it and asked, "Shall we schedule your procedure now?"

A procedure. That's all it was. A procedure. It was not an abortion or taking of a life. It was just a simple, common, everyday medical procedure. "Yes," I said quietly.

"How about Friday?" she asked. "Dr. Peterson will be doing them that day."

That soon? That was only three days away! I suddenly felt a bit dizzy. "I suppose," I found myself saying. She quickly typed it in, then wrote my appointment time on a card which she handed to me.

"See you Friday," she said with an encouraging smile.

I didn't respond but turned and walked like a zombie across the waiting room. The "Dearie" woman winked at me, but didn't say anything else.   As I approached the door I noticed one of the girls sitting next to an older woman who looked like her mother.   The girl was crying silently to herself, but her mother looked very stern. Shoving open the doors I took my leave of the accursed place, dropping my appointment card in a trash receptacle as I did so.   There was no way I was going to take evidence like that home for my folks to find.   I knew when my appointment time was, and didn't need a reminder.

Oh, how I hate this journal! I hate it! I hate it! I hate it! Why do I have to write how Jonathon was taken from me? Just to please my idiotic therapist? I won't do it! I refuse! Nothing can make me describe what happened at the end of those three days!

And yet here I am, describing it. I was a zombie.   For the next three days I walked around in a cloud as if I wasn't really alive. People talked to me and I did things and tried to act normal, but everything felt foggy and distant. It was as if I was looking at myself from far away as I went through the motions of everyday life.

I was in the same cloud when the call from Doctor Peterson came through the day before the appointment.   It came during lunch hour fortunately. I quickly grabbed Clarice and we headed out of the school lunch room and away from the school so no one would overhear.

Doctor Peterson spoke to me in a very kind voice and asked me lots of questions, wanting to make sure I wanted to do this, and that I understood I didn't have to do it, and that having the baby and giving it up for adoption was a very good option. There were, after all, many anxious parents who were dying to adopt.

But Bob had been on the warpath with me again the night before about how none of this could become known, and had dulled my mind so much that all I did was answer the doctor's questions like a robot. Yes, I knew what I was doing. No, I did not want to let the baby be born and offer it for adoption. Yes, I was aware that abortion could have an emotional impact upon me. No, I did not think it would be something too difficult for me to deal with. Yes, I was aware of the medical risks involved. No, I did not care to review any of the printed materials provided by the state regarding abortion.

It helped a lot that Clarice was there giving me support. We were sitting under an elm tree in the park across from the school. Her face was white as a sheet as she listened to the Doctor's questions and to my dull answers. The reason for her pallid look wasn't just because of the trauma she saw her best friend going through. Her own pregnancy self-test had finally come back positive just that morning. She would be facing a phone call like this herself very soon.

And then the call was over. I turned to Clarice with a questioning look in my eye. "Am I doing the right thing?" I mumbled stupidly. "Somehow, this doesn't feel right."

"It IS right!" Clarice assured me emphatically. "It's what you HAVE to do. You have no choice. It'll all be over soon, and then life will get back to normal and you'll forget all about it. You'll see."

"But Jonathon--"

"Don't give it a name!" cried Clarice, holding out her hands as if to ward off a blow. "It's just a blob of cells. That's all. It's NOT a life. Keep repeating that to yourself. They're just taking a few cells out of your body that you don't want anymore."

"I don't want them?" I repeated stupidly. "I don't want Jonathon? Why don't I want him?"

"We've been through this before," said Clarice in an exasperated tone. "You know the answers." She took my hand and roughly pulled me to my feet. "Let's get back to class and put this whole thing out of our minds." She yanked me along with her and headed back toward the school. But I noticed from the pinched look on her face that she was NOT putting the whole thing out of her mind. And frankly, neither was I.

And then the dreaded Friday came--and then the dreaded Friday passed. Like I said above, I simply cannot describe that day. Bob met me bricfly to give me the money, and then I went down to the clinic. The procedure was simple enough, and was indeed basically painless, although it was a little uncomfortable. There was a short time of recovery, and then I went home. But something happened that day that changed me forever. Those few cells that they took out of me must have contained not only Jonathon's life, but my own. Because my life ended that day, just as his did.

APRIL 22

This journal still lives! (unlike Jonathon) I did not throw it in the sewer after my therapy appointment as I'd planned. I tried to, and even found a particularly good sewer drain along the street to throw it into, where I could see the rushing, gurgling drain water, and could smell it a bit too. But for some reason, suddenly I just couldn't do it. I just couldn't throw the thing down there, even though I wanted to so badly.

And then all of a sudden I realized the reason. This journal is the only link I have to Jonathon, who has been gone for a year now. It is the only 'thing' I can look at and remember him by. And no matter how tortured and horrible the memory, I know I can never forget him. Not now, and not for eternity. I will forget my own existence before I will ever forget his.

But I'm off on a tangent again. The reality is, after the 'procedure' I went home feeling like a dead fish. I must have looked like one too since Mom wanted to put me straight to bed. "Are you sure you're all right?" she kept asking over and over, looking at me with big, worried eyes. Of course I always shrugged and said, "Yeah, I'm fine. Don't worry about me. I'm ok, really."

But she didn't believe me of course, and kept feeling my forehead and taking my temperature and then asking if anything was wrong again. Before long she convinced me I really WAS sick, and I ended up in bed for the rest of the weekend. In fact, I was still there on

Monday and Tuesday as well. My senior year in high school was ending soon and my classmates were all getting excited about graduation and the big parties that would go along with it, but all of that had become meaningless to me. All I could think about was Jonathon. Oscar tried constantly to get me to notice him by bumping up to me, wanting to be petted and fussed over. But I felt too depressed to do any such thing, and just ignored him.

Bob was ecstatic of course and kept calling on my cell to ask if I was getting better and to congratulate me on having done the abortion. "I am SO relieved you did it!" he kept saying over and over. His repeating this started to annoy me so I asked him at one point, "So, don't you even care at all about the baby that just died? He was yours too, you know."

There was silence on the other end of the line. Then he said simply, "There was no baby, and nothing just died. It was just a bunch of cells that were removed."

I suddenly felt very angry. Why did everyone keep saying that? If it really WAS just a blob of cells like a wart, why did I feel so terrible? I'd never felt bad about removing a wart before! Besides, no wart I'd ever known could grow fingers and toes, and have a brain. That 'blob of cells' business was starting to sound like a bunch of nonsense. And to say that it didn't die was also ridiculous. Even a removed wart dies. There was no question that what was pulled out of me was now dead, even though yesterday it was alive. And if I hadn't aborted it, it would STILL be alive!

"Well, you should care about the baby!" I blurted to Bob, suddenly wanting him to feel some of my pain. "He was your responsibility just as much as he was mine! And you decided to kill him too. It's the same as if you were there in the abortion clinic with me, having it done to you. How can you just sit back and treat it so casually? Don't you feel ANYTHING?"

He didn't give me a straight answer. He just stammered and mumbled after that, not sure what to say. Not long after that he hung up.

Clarice called later, and told me she was going on Tuesday to the abortion clinic to fill out her forms and make her appointment. She expected the abortion to happen on Friday, like mine. When she told me that, I choked up and couldn't say anything. I wanted to scream at her to not go, to spare herself the agony, but I couldn't seem to say a word. All I did was sit there balling, my tears dripping onto my cell phone. She heard it of course, and didn't know what to say. In the end our conversation sort of tapered off and she said she would call me later.

That was the longest, worst weekend I've ever spent in my life. And it was during that endless weekend--the very first night after the abortion, in fact--when the dreams started. Some people have recurring dreams that always repeat themselves and always come out the same way no matter how much you want them to change. My dreams are not like that. They are almost never the same, and sometimes they're full of sunshine, while other times there's just darkness. But there's always one thing about them that's the same. In every one of them Jonathon is there.

He never speaks to me of course. Sometimes when the dream is dark I don't even see him at all. But I always feel his presence. It's hard to describe how, really. All I know is that he's there, looking at me, watching me. Sort of like how a baby loves to watch its mother. When I first started having the dreams I sometimes yelled at him to go away, that he was just a blob of flesh like a wart and that he should stop staring at me. But he never moved. He always kept staring, never making a sound.

The most frightening dreams are the ones full of sunshine, since there is plenty of light in them to see Jonathon. And he has never been a mere blob of flesh in any of them. Always he looks the same--like a baby. I can see his tiny arms and hands, his teensy little toes, and his cute little blue eyes. Those eyes always stare at me adoringly, and when I first started having the dream I would either start screaming at him to stop staring, or tried to run away from him. But you know how it is when you run in a dream. It's like you're running in slow motion, and hardly moving at all. Jonathon somehow always followed me no matter how hard I ran, and seemed to get closer the farther I tried to go.

Sometimes there were knives in my dreams. Shiny, ugly, sharp knives that somehow I knew were abortion knives. Not that they use such knives in abortions, mind you. I frankly didn't know then what they used, and doubted it would be knives like these. But in my dreams, I somehow knew that these knives were 'dream' abortion knives, and were there for me to use on Jonathon. I always threw them away from him of course, as far as I could. But when I looked back at the table next to Jonathon, all the knives were there again.

Many times that first weekend I woke up in a cold sweat, and a few times I woke up screaming. Poor Mom wondered what on earth had happened to me. She even called Bob in the middle of the night to chew him out, since she thought my condition had been caused by a fight between him and me. Which I suppose in a way is true. Somehow it made me smile to think of her chewing him out in the middle of the night, and I slept a little bet afterward.

Mom insisted on taking me to a doctor on Monday. "Come on, honey," she wheedled. "There's obviously something wrong. Let's not get side tracked with a tangent--let's find out what the problem is, and then take care of it."

If only she knew! I'd already 'taken care of it'--indeed, THAT was the problem! I didn't want to go to a doctor of course, since I was afraid he might do a lot of tests and find out about my abortion. I tried to force my body to get better so I wouldn't have to go. But my body just wouldn't do it.

So on Monday afternoon we went to old Doc Jenkins, who's been our family doctor ever since I was born (he delivered me!) He looked me over and put a stick in my mouth making me say 'Aw,' and bumped the funny bone in my knee and took a blood and urine test, which he sent off to his lab. But when Mom asked him what was wrong he just shrugged his shoulders in confusion. "As far as I can tell," he said slowly, "she's showing the symptoms of what looks like post-traumatic stress."

Both he and Mom looked at me curiously, after which I got grilled with tons of questions about what had caused the traumatic stress.

"Did someone at school hit you?"

"Did you and Bob have a particularly bad fight?"

"Did you fall down a flight of stairs?"

"Did you and Bob have an awful fight?"

"Did you fall out of a tree house?"

"Did Bob tell you off, or hit you?"

"Did you nearly get hit by a school bus?"

Mom asked most of the questions of course, and most of her questions were about Bob. Naturally I told them nothing. But Mom didn't believe me of course, so she called up Bob again as soon as we left Doc Jenkins' office, and gave him another tongue lashing. Once more, it made me smile as I listened to her tear into him. It felt good to know that Bob was experiencing at least a little of the pain I was going through.

By Wednesday I was thankfully well enough to go back to school. As I walked down the familiar halls and saw the familiar smiling faces and goofy teachers, I felt totally like a zombie. It was as if I was a stranger here, looking through someone else's eyes at a world that didn't exist anymore. This place was not my school as it once had been. That was in a former life, before I died when Jonathon's blob of cells was removed.

To my surprise, Clarice was not in school that day. I suddenly realized that she hadn't called me back like she'd promised, and that five whole days had passed since we'd talked. I'd been too dead to the world to realize this before. So naturally I tried to get in touch with her. But no matter how often I texted her she didn't respond. That didn't help me of course, since I was starting to feel a desperate need to talk to someone, now that I was over being sick.

I talked to Bob at school, but he was no help as usual. He seemed genuinely confused about why I wasn't as happy and relieved as he was about the abortion. "What gives?" he demanded. "The things gone! It's not in you anymore! You should be ecstatic."

I just stared at him dumbly. "I don't feel very good about any of it. It still just doesn't feel right. And I keep having dreams about Jonathon."

Bob's face clouded over. "You're still giving it a name? Are you crazy? It was just a bunch of cells! Waste cells that you didn't want! You don't give your warts names, do you? Why do you care about something the size of a wart?"

"This wasn't a wart," I said with a frown. "It was Jonathon." Why was Bob so fixated on warts?

"Will you stop calling it by that name!" he yelled, causing several students down the hall to turn and stare. Then he started to chew me out for being ungrateful since he'd paid for it. He also chewed me out for the phone calls he'd got from my Mom. I just turned and walked away while he was still talking.

Thursday after school I went to Clarice's house since she still hadn't been in school and I wasn't able to reach her by texting. "She's not here," her dad told me when he opened the door. "She and her mom left yesterday to visit some relative in Florida that I didn't even know existed." He shook his head, apparently just as confused as I was. "Sounds like this relative is dying or something."

"Do you mind if I go look in her room?" I asked. Her dad just shrugged. Like Clarice's mom, he didn't much care if I came in, since I was at his house all the time. I dodged past him and trudged up to her room. Maybe there was some kind of clue about what had happened, since it just wasn't like Clarice to go this long without contacting me.

The mystery of why she hadn't answered my texts was instantly solved when I saw her phone by her bed. Obviously, future text and phone call attempts were pointless. But there was no other clue at all.

This was weird. Clarice had NEVER just gone off like this before. It crossed my mind that maybe her plan to have an abortion had been found out by her parents, and she was being punished for it. But her Dad wouldn't be acting the way he was if that was true. He'd be in a rage, instead of bumbling around his house in confusion. It just didn't add up.

I went home and tried to reach her on Facebook and gmail. But she never responded. Then I called the abortion clinic, since she'd said she was going in on Tuesday to fill out forms and make her abortion appointment. I thought maybe they could tell me what time her appointment was tomorrow. Who knows?

Maybe she'd come back for it. But the clinic just refused to give me any information, citing some privacy law I knew nothing about.

After that I texted her boyfriend Tom, but it turned out he was just as baffled as I was. She hadn't told him a thing about leaving, but had suddenly just disappeared.

I envied her. Somehow, she just disappeared. I wish I could do that. Oh, how I wish I could just vanish into thin air and make all this go away!

APRIL 24

Well, I'm back to this idiotic journal again. I hate it with a passion. I despise the sight of it, and have started cursing the day my stupid therapist told me to start keeping it. But somehow I keep feeling pulled to write in it, to finish my story. Maybe it's Jonathon that's pulling me. After all, this is his story as much as it is mine.

So, here goes. Back to the story which I wish I could forget, but can't stop thinking about or remembering. Friday came and went, and still no Clarice. One week had passed since Jonathon died at my hands. I marked the occasion by crying into my pillow half the night. Oscar tried to comfort me, but having my face licked by a sandpaper tongue was not very comforting.

The weekend that followed was a black hole that I hardly remember. It wasn't much better than the horrible weekend before. I honestly felt more dead than alive. I began wishing that our positions had been reversed, and that it was me that had been aborted, rather than Jonathon. At least then he would be alive.

Monday came and still no word from Clarice. However her Dad told me when I went to her house that her mom had called him over the weekend. But she didn't tell him much, just saying some vague thing about a dying relative. The poor man was starting to get really worried, not only about his daughter and wife and unknown relative, but about who was going to clean up the mess he'd made of his house since he'd thought she'd be back soon.

Life was going on for me, but it had NOT gone back to normal like Clarice said. Not at all. Like I said before, I felt more dead than alive. I had to drag myself through the days. I couldn't concentrate at school and completely stopped doing any homework. It all seemed so pointless. Mom was threatening to take me to another doctor, a specialist. I had little strength to resist her, even though I knew that could lead to real trouble. So she set up an appointment. Fortunately, it wasn't for another ten days, so I had some time to figure out an escape.

Meanwhile, I avoided Bob like the plague. The idiot was clueless as to why, and kept trying to text me. I finally shut off my phone. With Clarice gone, I hardly used it anyway.

And then on Wednesday my world exploded. And bad as I'd thought things were before, they suddenly got a whole lot worse. That's the way it is with life, I guess. Just when you don't think things can get any worse, they do.

APRIL 25

I know I should have kept going when I wrote the above, rather than just leave things with the unanswered question of what horrible thing happened on Wednesday. But no matter. No one but me will ever read this idiotic journal, and I know full well what happened. I just couldn't keep writing yesterday. Even though it's been a year, the memory is still too painful.

But for my moron therapist's sake, I'll keep going with the story. I feel a little stronger today, and think I can write it now. Then I can shove this journal in my therapist's face and yell, "See? I wrote the whole stinking story, and it hasn't helped me one bit!"

The minute I walked in the door after school that day and saw both Mom and Dad looking at me, I knew they'd found out about my abortion.

"Kate!" my Dad said in a voice that scared me. He was clenching and unclenching his fists, as if he was fighting to keep himself under control. "We received a report from Doctor Jenkins today. He got the results of the blood and urine tests you had last week. He says they suggest that you've recently ... had an abortion." He looked at me with eyes sparking fire. "Is that true?"

I could see his jaw muscles throbbing as if they would jump right off his face. The veins in his neck looked positively purple. The skin at the back of my own neck started to crawl, and I admit I was starting to feel downright frightened.

But when I glanced over at Mom, all of my fear melted away. If Dad looked scary, Mom looked out of this world. Her eyes were bloodshot, her hair was unkempt, and she was swaying on her feet as if she had been drinking or something. And she'd never touched alcohol in her life!

But it was her eyes that completely unnerved me. They were filled with more agony than I thought I could ever see in anyone's eyes. Those eyes which so often had loved and comforted me were now so swelled up with pain that I hardly recognized them. There was no accusation in those eyes, or anger of any kind. Just a deep and profound pain and horror that shocked me.

"Is this true?!" Dad repeated again, in a voice that sounded like thunder. I let my book bag slump to the floor and looked down at the carpet of our entry hall, fixing my eyes on the purple stain I'd caused at age ten when I spilled some grape juice. No matter how hard Mom had tried, she could never get that stain out. And it was starting to look like the stain of my abortion wouldn't go away either.

"Yes, it's true," I said softly. I braced myself for the nuclear blast I was sure would happen next. My Dad's temper could be a sight. He'd never struck me before, but it looked like that might be about to change. I closed my eyes for a second, waiting for the explosion to hit. And in the back of my mind, a stupid little voice sounded off like an annoying siren. "All that sneaking around to please Bob so that no one would know--and now they know! Was the abortion really necessary?"

But my surprises weren't over. To my shock, the only thing I heard next was my Dad letting out a long breath, as if he'd been socked in the stomach. Apparently my admitting the abortion had hit him harder than an actual fist. And as I looked up at him, I saw that his anger had died almost instantly. In its place was a haggard, weary look that made his face look a hundred years old.

What happened then was the longest, most awkward silence I had ever experienced with my parents in my life. No one said a word. We all just stood there, looking at each other. I kept waiting for Mom to rush in and offer comfort like she always had when I was hurt. But she didn't. And thinking about it, it was obvious why. THEY were the ones needing comfort, not me. I was the one who had hurt them.

But the trouble was, I needed comfort too. I was just a confused, stupid kid that had messed everything up badly. Never in my life had I felt more need for a kind word from my Mom. I knew I should say I was sorry. I knew I should beg for their forgiveness. I wanted to do just that, and even started to mouth the words. But for some reason my throat wouldn't work, and I just couldn't say anything. The emotions in that tiny entrance hall were so intense that no word would come out.

This was far worse than being yelled at, or even being hit. I suddenly found myself wishing my Dad WOULD explode like he'd been about to do, that he'd start yelling at me for not listening to him and not keeping my religious standards and letting things get out of hand with Bob, and then for aborting our baby. But as I looked at him, I saw that he was just as helpless and speechless as I was. Like me, he was too overcome with emotion to even talk.

But Mom was the worst. Her eyes still held more pain than I could ever remember seeing in anyone's eyes before. And then they slowly started to shift. The pain receded, and in its place came a glazed and lifeless look. Her mouth twitched, and she swayed dangerously on her feet. Then she started to fall--to collapse, really. Dad caught her of course.

"Mom!" I cried, looking down intensely into her face. She returned my gaze with a look of sheer horror. Then she tried to say something. She mouthed some words, but at first I couldn't understand what they were. Then she tried again, and this time I heard what she said.

"You stopped its heartbeat," she said simply, in a voice so strained it sounded like she was choking. "You stopped its heartbeat. They detect a heartbeat you know, about 25 days after conception, which is about the time you find out you're pregnant. You stopped it. You stopped its heart."

Then her eyes glazed over and she went completely limp. "Quick!" cried Dad. "Call Doc Jenkins!" I just stood rooted to the spot, Mom's words ringing in my ears. I had stopped Jonathon's heart. I had stopped Jonathon's heart. I had stopped Jonathon's heart!

"Don't just stand there!" cried Dad again. "She needs a doctor!"

Tears were suddenly blurring my vision. I turned and stumbled to the door, yanking it open. Then I lurched down our front walk and out toward the street. The blasted tears were starting to flood my eyes, and I couldn't see where I was going.

And then I was running. Running like the wind. Running just like in my dreams, knowing that Jonathon was right behind me, even though I'd stopped his heartbeat. Only this time my running was not in slow motion. I took off down our street like a rocket on fire.

APRIL 26

A year has passed since the events of that day. Most people would agree that a year is a long time. At least when we say "a year has passed" it sounds like a long time. After all, that's 365 days!

But the memory of that day is still etched so strongly in my mind, it's as if it just happened yesterday. And most of all my Mom's words "You stopped its heart" come back to haunt me, at the most unexpected of times. I can be casually doing something mundane, not thinking of my abortion or Jonathon at all, and suddenly her words leap into my mind. And then I start to shake all over and the horror of that day comes crashing back down around my ears.

With the passage of time over the last year, and as I've gotten a little older, I've realized that Mom's reaction was probably not a typical one. Many mothers in a moment like that when they clearly perceived their daughter was in so much pain and trauma would have said something comforting. They would have set aside their own horror and tried to lovingly comfort their daughter. The maternal instinct would have kicked in to see their child suffering, and they would have tried to comfort rather than yell or freak out. After a minute or two of comforting, THEN they would have started to yell and freak out. But even then, probably the last thing they would do is to say something about how their daughter stopped the baby's heart when she had an abortion. They would know that would just make their daughter feel far worse.

No, my Mom's reaction was probably not a typical one. But as I was soon to learn, there was a reason for her reaction. A very understandable reason, too. But it was not an easy or a painless one, as I was to discover.

And anyway, who am I to make such judgments about how a mother should respond? After all, I stopped Jonathon's heartbeat! I made no effort as a mother to comfort Jonathon in his moment of need, and he was in a state of far greater innocence and pain than I was that day in our front hall. Can I really blame Mom for her first reaction, when I acted with far more callousness toward my own child? Seriously, who am I to judge?

Of course, some people--like the "Dearie" lady at the abortion clinic--might scoff at my saying this, and point out that my abortion was simply to remove a growth of cells, and that I was not really a "mother" like my own Mom at all. Therefore, they say, I should not feel bad about what I did to Jonathon because there was no Jonathon to feel bad about.

I no longer believe such complete and utter nonsense. He had a HEARTBEAT for cat's sake! Is a being with a heartbeat and DNA different than mine really just a blob of worthless cells, like a wart or a cancerous growth? Don't give me that rot! He was MY baby, and I killed him! What Mom said that day helped me to finally understand that. And also to finally understand that there was no justification--absolutely NO justification--for what I had done. Would I walk casually by and watch a man bleed to death on the sidewalk? No. I would recognize him as a human in need and try to help him. Why did I do differently with Jonathon?

That whole business of a "woman's body" and a woman's right to do with "her body" what she wants is sheer lunacy. Jonathon's body was not my body. His body was dependent on mine, but only briefly, for a few months--just like some people become briefly dependent on life support machines, and others depend on donors to give them a kidney to stay alive. Men fighting in wars do things with their bodies they don't want to do. They suffer for a few months so that others who are innocent can live in peace. So do policemen and firemen. Many average men go to jobs they hate and subject their bodies to abuse to feed their families. Have the women of this world descended so far down the road of selfishness they no longer see any need to experience some discomfort to save someone's life? Why was I so selfish that I put my own comfort and fear of being found out as a higher priority and more important than Jonathon's existence?

The truth is, Jonathon's DNA makeup was so different from mine that if it had been found at an explosion crime scene where a few bits of DNA were all that was left of him and me, he would have been identified as a separate, distinct human being--not as part of me at all! NO DNA expert would have identified him as being part of my body.

And that whole business of his not being a 'life' or 'alive' is also sheer stupidity. Of course he was alive! If he were dead tissues, my body would have expelled him! And while he wasn't a fully grown human being like me, he had every bit as much individuality in his few tiny cells as I do in my few billion cells. His brain was there, his heart, his arms and hands and feet--all of it was there, fully developed in genetic code that just needed a little time to develop physically. This was no stray group of random, worthless and useless cells. This was no wart. This was a person, plain and simple.

But I'm getting off on a tangent again. I'm getting ahead of my story. I have to calm down and pull myself back to that horrid day when Mom and Dad found out and I went running crazily down the street instead of calling the Doctor like I should have done. Because once again, I was just thinking about ME, rather than someone else that needed me. Someone else like Jonathon or Mom. After all, Mom could have been having a seizure or a heart attack there in the hall. And did I help her? No. So once more, rather than act to save the life of someone who needed me, I tried to simply escape, leaving them to die.

It seemed like I ran for hours. I ran until my breath came in ragged gasps that threatened to tear my ribs apart. I was gulping air like a hooked fish gulps for water. I paid no attention to where I was going, since I had lost all touch with everything around me. It's a wonder I didn't get hit by a car.

When I finally came to my senses, I found myself in a city park, with a couple of old guys sitting on a park bench staring at me. They had good reason, too. Looking down into the park's duck pond, I saw that my hair was wild and straggly, my face was streaked with tears and smeared with make-up, and my eyes were bloodshot and bulging.

"You all right?" called out one of the men to me. I simply nodded in reply, still gasping for air from my long run. "You don't look it," he said again, which I suppose he thought was supposed to help somehow. It didn't, of course.

As I stood there being stared at by the two old dudes, I came to one of the great and very simple realizations of my life. No matter how hard you try to run away from a thought you don't like, you can't do it. I'd run like crazy, but my Mom's words "You stopped its heart" still echoed through my mind. And no matter how hard I tried, I simply could not make those words go away.

I'd stopped Jonathon's heartbeat! Why hadn't anyone told me he had a heartbeat at 25 days? He had a HEART for crying out loud--and I'd stopped it from beating! This was no blob of cells gone wild, no mere wart. Warts don't have hearts, and neither do cancerous growths. He had a HEART, and I'd stopped it! ME. I had killed him!

I put my hands over my eyes and began to sob like a moronic baby. "You sure you're all right?" called out one of the old dudes behind me stupidly. I didn't answer, since if he had any brains he'd know the answer. I just dropped to my knees, sinking partway into the water of the pond, and balled and sobbed like I'd never balled and sobbed before. You'd think another flood was on the way, with the amount of water that gushed out of my eyes.

"I don't think she's all right," I heard one of the old dudes behind me say.

"What do we do about it?" asked his companion.

"Beats me," came the response. "I've been married almost 50 years, and I never HAVE figured out how to make 'em stop crying once they get started."

His statement was so utterly ridiculous, the bizarre part of my personality was strongly tempted to start laughing. But the horror of what I had done to Jonathon was still too great. I continued to sob and blubber, falling flat on the grass next to the pond. I must have looked like I was dying.

"Think we should call a paramedic?" asked the second man.

"There's nothin' they could do," answered the first man. "They'd probably just sit here and stare at her like we're doin.'"

I suddenly knew I had to get out of here. The comments of those two men were getting to be too much for me. With tremendous effort I staggered to my feet. As I did so I caught a glimpse of myself in the pond. The sight was shocking. My eyes were even more puffy and bulged now and my make-up was so smeared it looked like a kindergartner's finger painting. In fact, my whole face looked like it had just been kicked by a mule.

"You SURE you're all right, young lady?" asked the first old gentlemen for the third time.

"Of course," I blubbered in a barely intelligible voice as I staggered away. "Why wouldn't I be?"

I quickly (and gratefully) left the two staring men behind me. But as I staggered along I found myself wondering just where I was supposed to go now. After all, if you can't go home, where can you go? My overloaded brain had a hard time puzzling that one out, but I just kept putting one foot in front of the other and kept going just the same. And after 5 minutes my brain finally realized where my feet were taking me. I was going to Bob's house.

Bob. I grimaced suddenly, making my face look even worse (if that was possible). He was the cause of all this! If it wasn't for him, none of this would have ever happened! It was him and his stupid antics on dates, and his insistence that I have an abortion! Yet even as these angry words spat across my mind, I knew they were only partially true. Bob could never have caused any of this without my consent. I'd knowingly gone along with him every step of the way. It made me feel better to put all the blame on him, but deep down inside I knew it wasn't true.

Before I knew it, I found myself on Bob's front doorstep. My mind was too far gone to consider what his Mom or Dad would say when they caught sight of me. Fortunately I never found out. Bob himself answered the door.

"Kate!" he cried in alarm the instant he saw me. "What's happened to you?" I stared at him helplessly for a minute, then found myself dissolving into tears once more. Drat those tears! I couldn't seem to make them stop! I felt like an idiot standing on his doorstep crying like a two-year-old. Bob must have realized his neighbors might think it odd, so he quickly pulled me inside and shut the door.

"My parents aren't home right now, thank heavens," he said as he led me over to the couch. "You've got to get a grip on yourself. What's wrong? What's happened?" The concern in his voice touched my heart, which unfortunately caused a new flood of tears. Why had I ever doubted Bob would comfort me? He may be thickheaded at times, but he truly cared about me. So of course I should turn to him, since he surely would understand what I was going through.

"My parents know," I blubbered in a whiny sort of voice that probably sounded very irritating. "They know!"

Bob was off the couch as if his pants were on fire. "THEY KNOW!" he blared. "Why did you tell them? Don't you have any sense at all? Now they'll tell MY parents!"

Anger suddenly took the place of tears, as my face twisted into a nasty grimace. "I did NOT tell them, you idiot! They found out! And my Mom had a breakdown and probably died right there in the hall! And my Dad looked like he was going to hit me, and then he just looked old and half dead!"

Bob stared at me with a frenzied look in his eyes, apparently not having heard a word I said. "They'll tell my parents!" he repeated dumbly, as if that was the only thing that mattered in the world. "They'll tell MY PARENTS!"

"Well, so what?" I bellowed. "You can't always have what you want, and you can't always keep secrets. Especially about something like this. So LIVE WITH IT!"

He apparently still hadn't heard me. He was just wandering stupidly around the room, clenching and unclenching his fists (which must be a 'guy' thing), muttering, "They'll tell my parents! THEY'LL TELL MY PARENTS!"

I suddenly realized that any notion Bob could comfort me was seriously mistaken. At the moment, he looked more like he was about to jump out the window, or start hitting me, or do something else insane and stupid. It was only too obvious the last thing he was capable of doing right now was comforting anyone.

"Why did this happen?" he suddenly yelled, slamming his fist into the fireplace, which must have hurt. "Now the whole world is going to know! Why did you have to go and get pregnant? Why? If you had any sense, you'd have done something to prevent it! Like most girls I've dated in the past who have brains! They all were on the pill or used the patch, or something. They never got pregnant! But NO! You have to go and do NOTHING and then get pregnant. How's a guy supposed to have any fun with a stupid girl like that? An idiot girl who doesn't even have enough sense to--"

"STOP IT!!" I suddenly shrieked at the top of my voice, surprising even myself. What he was saying was so sick and disgusting that it took a

~ 53 ~

supreme effort of willpower to not lash out and slap him in the face. I saw for the first time where his mind was, what he truly thought of me, and what the whole thing had really been all about. Other girls! He had done this to other girls! Just using them like toys, for his pleasure! I suddenly felt like I was going to throw up.

Bob was so startled by my unexpected scream that he took an involuntary step backward, tripping over the lamp table. Spinning around to catch his balance he smacked his nose onto the mantle of the fireplace, instantly spattering blood everywhere. It got all over the carpet and furniture, and also on the family pictures on the mantle. Bob staggered sideways in shock and tripped again, over a chair this time. He landed flat on his back. For a minute he made no sound, staring at the ceiling with wide eyes. Then he started to whine and cry like a little two-year-old, tears mixing with the blood that was pouring out of his nose.

"You moron!" he wailed through his tears. "Look at what you did to me! How am I going to explain THIS to my folks when they come home? And my nose! It hurts! Because of you it's probably broken! JUST LOOK WHAT YOU DID TO ME!"

The sight of the blood had somehow sapped all of the intense emotion that had been surging through me only seconds before. Suddenly I felt very cold. I looked down at Bob, feeling no compassion at all. Indeed, for all the balling and emotion I'd just been through, I suddenly felt amazingly calm and clear headed.

"Wrong, Bob," I said coolly. "Just look at what you did to yourself."

Then I turned and walked away, knowing it was over between him and me forever. And good riddance, too.

APRIL 28

I spent the night at Clarice's house, since I couldn't bring myself to go home. I was so exhausted and confused and horrified and disgusted with everything that had happened, I just needed somewhere to try and recover. I didn't actually intend to spend the night there, and was thinking I might have to go to the homeless shelter or use a park bench. But things just sort of worked out for me to stay there instead.

Not that Clarice was there, of course. She and her mother were still gone to Florida when I went there after leaving Bob's house. Her Dad answered the door as usual. It's incredible he didn't seem to notice my smeared, pudgy face with all of its tear streaks, or the spray of Bob's nose-blood that covered one of my pant legs.

"Sorry Kate," he blustered, throwing the door open for me, then instantly turning and racing off into the house. "But I've got a plane to catch in an hour! To Florida! I've had enough of my wife's dodgy answers about this mysterious relative who's supposed to be dying. So, I'm going down there myself to find out what's going on!" He disappeared into the kitchen where he yelled, "You can go on up to Clarice's room again if you want to, and stay as long as you want! Just lock the door when you leave!"

Five minutes later he was gone, gunning down the street in his old station wagon in an effort to make it to the airport on time.

And to tell you the truth, he wasn't the only one who hoped he'd make it. Like I said before, I was a basket case and just needed somewhere to crash, and Clarice's house fit the bill perfectly. If he DIDN'T make his plane he'd be back of course, and then I'd have to leave. I waited anxiously, watching the street from Clarice's upstairs window for what must have been an hour, using all my willpower to drive all other thoughts from my mind except the question of whether he'd made his plane. I knew I had to keep out all other thoughts in case he came back, since I simply could not afford to lose control in front of him.

Finally I decided he must have made his flight. I now had the house to myself, at least for the time being. But now, without anything for my mind to concentrate on, Mom's words came back to me full force once more. Without even bothering to wash the smears off my face I flopped down on Clarice's bed and just lay there, sobbing helplessly once again. It was the same old, familiar bed that she and I had jumped and played on ever since we were little kids, and somehow it felt soft and comforting.

But no amount of softness or comfort could erase my mother's words that kept leaping back into my mind. "You stopped its heart! You stopped its heartbeat! You stopped its heart!"

Before I knew it I was smearing Clarice's pillow with my tears and streaky makeup. My hand was throbbing from where I'd belted Bob, but I didn't care. What was a little pain, anyway? I'd stopped a heartbeat! Surely that was far more painful!

The sudden realization made me sit up on the bed. Did Jonathon feel much pain when I stopped his heart? How much did it hurt him? How much WOULD it hurt, to have your heart stop? And how could a living being with a heartbeat not feel pain? The enormity of these questions seized my mind, and I flopped back down, balling again for all I was worth. I had caused so much pain! ME! I had done it! I had forced Jonathon to experience agony and then death. There are no words to describe how low and disgusting this made me feel.

Time drifted by in the odd way it does when we lose track of reality. I must have dozed eventually, sometime after my tears dried up and I found it hard to cry anymore. I vaguely remember waking up and being surprised to see it was dark outside. Why was it dark? What was I doing in Clarice's room? Why wasn't I home in my own bed, with Oscar nuzzling up to me and trying to wake me up like usual?

And then the memory crashed around my ears as Mom's words once more echoed in my head. "You stopped its heart! You stopped its heart! You stopped its heart!" I found that my tear fountain had refilled, so Clarice's pillow was once more subjected to a salty deluge. I had never known I could feel so low or disgusting, or so completely worthless as a human being. After a long time, I mercifully dozed again.

And then it was morning. A stupid bird was chirping away annoyingly at the window, with a sound that pounded in my dull brain like a power drill. I sat up suddenly and looked around. Once again I experienced a minute of disorientation, wondering what I was doing in Clarice's room. Then of course, reality came back to me once more, as did Mom's echoing words in my head.

But I knew I couldn't just lie here and cry forever. Mom and Dad must be worried about me, since I'd stayed out all night. I'd never done that before. I hastily grabbed my bag and pulled out my phone, starting to dial. Only then did I discover why I had not heard any of the many phone calls they had no doubt tried to make to me through the night. My battery was dead.

I went over to Clarice's phone and started to dial. Her battery was nearly gone too, but it looked like it had just barely enough juice in it to make one call. I had nearly dialed all the numbers when I suddenly hesitated. The image of Mom's horrified, agonized eyes came into my mind, along with the sight of my Dad's haggard face.

I dropped the phone with a clatter. I couldn't call them. Not now. I knew I would have to eventually, but I just felt too weak to call right now. I just couldn't handle it.

There was another reason for my weakness. I'd had no food since lunch yesterday in the school cafeteria, and even then I'd just picked at my food since I wasn't hungry. I headed for the stairs to go down to the kitchen, but stopped when I caught a glimpse of myself in Clarice's bathroom mirror.

What a sight! My hair looked like it had been supercharged to stand straight up on end by multiple doses of electricity. My face was so blotchy and streaked and swollen it looked like the belly of a fat zebra. My eyes were bloodshot, and my makeup had smeared and shifted around so much it gave my face the appearance of a circus clown.

So, for the next hour, I finally took care of myself and tried to repair the damage. I showered and then borrowed some of Clarice's clothes to wear (she wouldn't mind, and fortunately we were the same size). Then, noticing her streaked pillowcase and quilt I had messed up so badly last night, I took them down to be washed. I was disturbed to find a pile of dirty socks and other clothes belonging to Clarice's Dad on top of the washing machine, which the poor man had been clueless about how to wash. I threw in the whole load.

After that I spent the next hour washing all the dishes he had amazingly dirtied since Clarice's mother left (every dish in the house-- some of them multiple times!) and cleaned the kitchen. And then as if that weren't enough, I went on a real cleaning binge, going through the house and doing all the chores Clarice's mother usually did. Somehow mundane tasks such as washing and cleaning brought a feeling of normalcy back into my dull mind, and helped push out the horror of the last day.

But one cannot clean forever. And by mid afternoon I had done all I could do. Mom's words "You stopped his heartbeat" started jumping around in my mind again, and I knew I couldn't just sit there and watch TV. I also knew I wasn't quite ready to go home yet, or even to call.

What was I to do? School was almost over for the day. Clarice was obviously not home, so I couldn't see her. I would NEVER be seeing Bob again. I wasn't as close to my other friends, and didn't dare just show up at their house, since I knew they'd ask all kinds of questions about why I'd missed so much school lately, and why I'd been acting so dead when they saw me in the halls.

So what was I to do? Where was I to go? Who could I turn to? My pastor? No. He would instantly tell my parents, and I wasn't ready for that. Aunt Minnie in Monroeville? No. She would just call up Dad.

I'm not sure when the idea first came into my mind. It was a crazy idea, really. But in a way it wasn't crazy. It was the last place in the world I should have thought of going, yet in a bizarre sort of way, it was the most logical place for me to visit in light of all that had happened. After all, that doctor who'd called me before my abortion had seemed very kind and caring. Of course I'd left my car at home so I'd have to catch a bus to get there. But there were plenty of buses.

I grabbed my purse and headed out the door, my mind fixed on going down to the abortion clinic.

APRIL 29

If anyone other than me ever was to read this stinking journal, they'd think I have a sick mind. Why on earth would I go back to the scene of the crime? Why go to the abortion clinic where Jonathon was taken from me-- where I'd stopped his heartbeat? You'd think that would be the last place in the world I'd want to go.

But somehow, I was simply drawn to it. Maybe it was Jonathon, pulling me. Maybe it was a morbid sense of wanting to engage in self-torture by going back to the place where I'd done the most awful thing of my life.

Or maybe, just maybe, I was simply searching for understanding and sympathy from people who shared my experience, and who knew about it. And I had no idea where else to find such people.

It took a lot longer to get there on the bus than it did when I drove my car--almost two hours! But I had nothing better to do, and nowhere else to go so time really didn't matter anyway. I just sat on the bus, staring blankly out the window, seeing nothing. I tried my best to keep my mind from repeating what Mom had said about stopping Jonathon's heart, but it wasn't easy. I counted stop signs, red cars, out-of-state license plates, and even garbage on the side of the road in an effort to keep my mind busy and away from those awful words.

And finally I was there. This time I didn't fuss or delay going in once I got there. I just walked right up and blazed in the door. My mind was too dazed to care anymore about appearances, so I felt no shame as dozens of women's eyes turned on me as I entered.

"Can I help you?" asked the receptionist at the desk. Her simple smile made me feel better already, even though she was a different receptionist than before.

"I'd like to talk to someone about my abortion," I said simply.

She looked at me, confused. "You mean you want to talk to someone about having one?"

"No, I've already had one," I said quickly, starting for the first time to feel a bit self conscious since everyone in the reception room was hearing every word I said. "I just want to talk to someone about it."

She was still mystified. "Has there been an allergic reaction?" she asked. "Or do you want to talk about your bill?"

"No, there's no reaction," I said in growing exasperation. "And the bill's been paid. I just wanted to talk about it. You know--about how to make sense of it, and everything."

Now she understood. "Oh, I see," she said, looking down at her desk in momentary confusion. "Let me check with one of the nurses here and get back to you. Just have a seat. It won't be long."

I scanned the room, looking for a seat as far away from everyone else as possible. I didn't want another "Dearie" lady talking to me and telling me about how wonderful an abortion was. Most eyes in the room looked at me with curiosity. No one said anything as I took a seat and grabbed a magazine to read while I waited.

I suppose it should have occurred to me to open up to these people and tell them what I had learned about abortions. I should have told everyone there in the waiting room about my abortion experience, and about how they should change their minds and not go through with it. It would have been the perfect opportunity. But as usual, I was so fixated on ME and my problems that I didn't even think of this. My mind was focused on only one thing--talking to someone who could help me feel better. There was no room left in my brain for any other constructive thought.

Minutes passed. I found it hard to concentrate on my magazine, especially since mom's statement about Jonathon's heartbeat kept echoing back into my mind. I felt impatient that it was taking so long for them to find someone I could talk to. After all, how hard of a request was that?

I took a peek around my magazine at the other people in the reception room. As before, it was mostly filled up with young girls about my age, some of them unhappily sitting next to their mothers. There were also a few older women. No one looked very pleased to be there, and the deadness in everyone's eyes was depressing.

Suddenly the door opened, letting in a cool breeze. We all looked up to see a middle-aged lady enter the room. She was shabbily dressed and had rather heavy doses of makeup all over her face. From the way she was swaying on her feet, she had obviously been drinking.

The lady teetered over to the reception desk. "May I help you?" the receptionist asked, trying to pull back from the smell of alcohol that rolled off the woman.

"I'm here for my abortion," the lady said loudly. "Time to get this baby out!"

"Your name please?"

"Dorothy Malk. I hope the Doc's more careful this time. In my last abortion, I felt a pinch."

"Just have a seat please."

Dorothy Malk looked around the waiting room. I felt my heart sink as she spotted a seat next to me and headed for it.

"Hey, toots, this seat taken?" she asked as she sat next to me, the scent of alcohol descending on me like a fog. It was obvious there was no need to reply, since she was already sitting there and didn't look like she intended to move. I therefore chose to ignore her and pretended to be intently interested in my magazine.

"Glory be, it'll be wonderful to get rid of the brat inside me," Dorothy said huskily. "I don't like it when I feel him kick."

I was so shocked by this statement, I found myself blurting, "You can feel him kick? But that must mean you're at least four months along!"

"True enough, toots!" hooted Dorothy. "I'm five months. Didn't have any money for an abortion in the first trimester, so I had to wait 'till now. Too bad, since it's more expensive. But I got the money at last, and they still do them this late. On my last pregnancy I waited almost SIX months! Squeaked in just under Pennsylvania's 24 week deadline." She added this last piece of information with a bit of pride. I stared at her aghast. The idea of having an abortion when you could feel the baby moving was unthinkable.

"Oh, that last abortion was a beauty, it was," said Dorothy. "You know, they usually use suction for abortions under 3 months, which pulls so strong it shreds the baby to pieces and pulls it out in bloody clumps. Then they reach in and scrape out the remaining pieces with a curved tool, kind of like a knife. That's pretty simple. But after 3 months, it gets more interesting."

I suddenly wanted to throw up. Is that what they had done with Jonathon? Suctioned him out like he was a piece of garbage? My stomach started to churn as if I'd just found out I'd been served rat meat at a restaurant.

"You see, a suction won't work when the brat gets too big. They got to reach in and crush his skull like an egg, then pull him out piece by piece if he doesn't come in one yank. But my last baby was so big and I was so far advanced they had to do a special job. They had to pull him partway out--partial birth, they call it--then stab scissors into his little skull to make a hole. Then they stuck a tube into the hole and suctioned out his brains. After that his skull collapsed easy enough, and they were able to pull out the rest of the pieces with no trouble. It was a bit bloody, but aren't they all?"

A girl across from me threw up. The sight of it caused a chain reaction and three others in the reception room joined her. But of course, the primary reason for the reaction was not just the sight of throw up. It was Dorothy's horrific, vivid description. I was so shocked my mind was reeling from the ghastly enormity of what she had said. She'd described the bloody mutilation of a helpless infant as if it was nothing more than scooping out ice cream!

"Hey, what's the matter, toots?" bellowed Dorothy, seeing the horrified look on my face. "It's just a procedure to take out unwanted tissue. No need to get excited. It's perfectly legal and safe. Although last time I felt a pinch. And they had all the little arms and legs and fingers in this bowl not far away where I could see it, and--"

I shot up out of my chair and raced for the door. I was not alone. Half of those in the waiting room apparently decided they'd come back later and bolted to get out as well. There was momentary confusion as nearly ten of us tried to stuff ourselves through the door at once. Behind me I heard the receptionist and a nurse arguing with Dorothy, telling her she was drunk and would have to come back later when she would not upset the other patients.

But it was too late, of course. The other patients were already upset. The ten of us at the door finally made it out, and then went our respective ways. And I have a strong suspicion that at least one of those other girls had a change of heart, and went to term with her baby, forgetting forever about having an abortion.

As for me however, it was too late. I didn't have that blessed option anymore. And now in addition to Mom's words about stopping his heartbeat echoing through my mind, I had Dorothy's rough voice echoing as well. "They usually use suction ... which pulls so strong it shreds the baby to pieces."

APRIL 30

Why am I still writing in this stinking journal? What possible motive could I have to torture myself by continuing this horrible account about how I killed Jonathon? Because that's what I did to him. I killed him. Stone dead. I stopped his heartbeat, and then they suctioned him out ...

But I'm getting off on a tangent again. I have another therapy appointment in two days, and my therapist made me PROMISE I'd get my whole story written by then. Well, I probably won't make it. I can only write so much in here before I become so repulsed and disgusted I have to leave and go do something else. How I wish Oscar hadn't run away! His furry purring always helped cheer me up. But he's gone too, and there's nothing I can do to bring him back, except hope he comes back on his own.

Which is more than Jonathon can do. Nothing will bring him back. No amount of prayers or saying "I'm sorry, I didn't mean it!" or crying or self torture will bring him back. He's gone forever, because of what I did. And oh, how I wish--HOW I WISH--I could go back in time and undo everything, and bring him back. But I can't, of course. You can't change time or your past choices. All you can do is try to forgive and live with them. And sometimes that's pretty hard. In fact, sometimes it's impossible.

I finally went home that evening. Somehow Dorothy's words had galvanized my sense of guilt, so I knew I had to at least try to make amends with Mom and Dad. It was too late to make amends with Jonathon of course.

The minute I walked in the door I heard a kitchen chair scrape back and Dad came running into the front hall. "Kate!" he yelled as he saw me. "Thank goodness you're back!" Then he scooped me up and hugged me like he's never hugged me before. I was so shocked, I didn't know what to do. This was not the reaction I'd expected! I'd thought he was going to blow his top!

I suddenly felt something wet on my shoulder. In amazement, I realized my Dad was crying, his tears spilling onto my jacket. My Dad never cried! Even at Grandma's funeral he'd never shed a tear! But now from the shower that was falling onto my shoulder, it was obvious he'd had a change of heart.

"Oh, Kate!" he said, pulling back and looking at me intensely. "Thank goodness you came back. I've been so worried about you!" The look in his eye was almost half crazed. Guilt stabbed my heart as I realized what I'd put him through.

"Where's Mom?" I stammered, not knowing what else to say or do. A momentary flash of pain crossed Dad's eyes.

"Upstairs, in bed," he said flatly. "Doc Jenkins is up there now, checking on her." His jaw muscles started to twitch. It was obvious he'd been going through tremendous stress. But rather amazingly, his eyes didn't hold any accusation or anger toward me at all. Just relief that I was there.

And then he unexpectedly hugged me again. "Oh Kate," he said softly in my ear while he squeezed the life out of me. "I never want to lose you. Never again. I wouldn't be able to go on. That would be the end."

Tears were dropping on my shoulder again. Suddenly a few of my own began to drop as well. And then both of us melted in a mutual tear fest that once more reduced me to a blubbering mess. I wasn't sure how much more of this crying business I could take!

But the sight of my Dad crying was what did it. He never cried like this! And emotional as I've been lately, something in the back of my mind told me there was something about this whole picture that didn't quite add up. If Mom's reaction the other day had been a bit strange, there was no question this reaction from my Dad was strange also. This was as unlike him as if he'd suddenly decided to join the Mafia and become a hit man.

A sudden noise on the stairs behind us brought us back to our sobbing senses. It was Doc Jenkins coming down. He looked grave, but at the sight of me he cheered up considerably. "Kate!" he called. "How wonderful to see you! And I think you might be just the therapy Carol needs right now. At least I hope so. Come on up with me!"

He took me by the hand and pulled me up the stairs. "Is Mom ok?" I managed to mumble as I tried to bring my tear ducts back under control.

"Um, not bad," he responded vaguely. "She's resting comfortably, and I'm sure she'll be delighted to see you." He led me eagerly toward the bedroom at the end of the upstairs hall, Dad close on our heels. And then without any preliminary, he fairly pushed me in the door.

"You've got a visitor, Carol," he announced with a grand smile. "Look! It's Kate! She's come back!"

I stared blankly at Mom's pasty, white face on her pillow. Her blank eyes just looked at me curiously, as if I was a menu she was examining at a restaurant. Her hands lay limply on the sheet and she looked almost as if she was dead. Even her eyes held very little life, and certainly lacked the sparkle they always used to have.

"Kate," said my Mom in a hollow voice. "Kate. Is that really my Kate? Really and truly?"

"It sure is!" announced Doc Jenkins. A feeling of horror was starting to rise up from the pit of my stomach. She wasn't talking at all like her normal self. Did she even recognize me? What had happened to her?!

"My Kate," repeated Mom with a faint smile. "My little Katydid." My heart leaped at these words, since that's what Mom used to call me when I was a little girl. But even as this relief started to rise up within me, her next words shattered everything.

"I used to have a girl named Kate. Only she died. She died."

My eyes big as saucers, I stared at her, then at Doc Jenkins, then at Dad. The men both looked grave, and Doc Jenkins was shaking his head sadly. "I had hoped it would work," he mumbled softly.

"What's wrong with her?" I yelled suddenly. "What's happened? What did you hope would work?" Tears were coming into my eyes again, and a new wave of guilt threatened to reduce me to a blubbering mass of sobbing once more.

"Paul, I wonder if you could run down and get this prescription for me," said Doc Jenkins unexpectedly, pulling a piece of paper from his pocket. "That will give me a chance to talk to Kate for a few minutes alone."

Dad gave him a long look. "Are you sure?" he said for no good reason that I could understand. "I'm her father, so I should be the one--"

"No, no, I think this is best," said Doc Jenkins. "Just take your time with that prescription."

By now my eyes were so wide they threatened to pop out of my head. "What's going on?" I bellowed. "What are you going to talk to me about? And what's wrong with Mom?"

Before I could answer, Mom spoke up again. "Kate? Kate? Is that you?"

Turning I cried out, "Yes Mom! I'm here!"

She was looking right at me, but didn't seem to see me. "Kate! Oh, Kate! I didn't mean to do it! Really I didn't! Paul was so insistent though! And it didn't seem like I had any choice. I'm so sorry, Kate! So sorry!" There was pleading in her voice. Agonized pleading, as if she was begging me for forgiveness.

"I don't understand!" I yelled at her. "What are you saying?"

She looked at me with glazed eyes. Then she said, "I used to have a girl named Kate. Little Katydid. But she died. She went away. I never got to see her." Tears were welling up in her unseeing eyes.

Doc Jenkins pulled gently on my arm. "Come downstairs for a minute Kate. There are a few things I need to tell you."

I turned on him with fire in my eyes. "What have you done to Mom?" I shouted nonsensically. "What's happened to her?"

"Kate," said Dad, taking my other arm and steering me gently but firmly toward the door. "Let's leave Mom for a few minutes. I've got to fill this prescription. Doc Jenkins will explain everything."

Dumbly I allowed myself to be half pushed, half dragged down the stairs. I had a sudden urge to start screaming and ranting and raving, demanding to be told what was happening. The only reason I didn't was because I'd started shaking so bad I had to concentrate on the stairs, so I wouldn't stumble and then roll all the way to the bottom.

At the front door, Dad turned to look at me. There was a profound sense of sadness in his tired eyes. And then he said something that made no sense at all.

"Don't judge me too harshly, Kate. I've changed. I never want to lose you again."

I just stared at him, not comprehending. He sighed heavily, then went out the door.

"Come here into the living room Kate, and let me tell you a story," said Doc Jenkins, in a voice that I could tell was an attempt at being cheerful.

"I don't want to hear a story!" I yelled. "I want to know what's wrong with Mom!" I moved toward the stairs, heading back up to see her again.

"But this story IS about your mother," said Doc Jenkins. "And about your father too. It's a true story. I think it will help explain things, so you can have a better idea about what's going on."

I turned back toward the living room and stared at him. Then slowly I walked over and sat down. A deep sense of foreboding was starting to rise up in my chest. First the horror of what I had done to Jonathon, and now this! I didn't think I could take much more of this!

Doc Jenkins smiled at me. It was a rather lopsided smile, since it was obvious he didn't feel like smiling. I suddenly found myself wondering why HE was telling me this story, instead of Mom or Dad. None of this made any sense.

"A long time ago--around 19 years ago to be exact--there was a young doctor, just starting off his practice," he said dryly.

"You?" I asked.

He shrugged. "Let's just say it was a young doctor. He'd been in general practice for a few years. However, he decided to add a new specialty to his doctor services. It was an up-and-coming specialty for a doctor to take in that day, although it was a bit controversial. You see, this doctor decided he would start doing abortions."

My heart froze as if it had been stabbed by an icicle. Here we were back to hated abortions again. Why couldn't I ever escape from them?

"What are you talking about?" I blurted. "I thought we were talking about Mom and what's wrong with her! Why are you telling me some nonsense about a doctor who was stupid enough to start doing abortions?"

"I was about to explain that," he said unruffled. "You see, one day a young woman came to see him--came to have an abortion, actually. And this young woman's name was Carol Brown--soon to be changed to Carol Anderson, when she married your father."

MAY 1

I feel sick. Not just troubled sick or emotionally sick, but physically sick. I'd thought telling the disgusting details of my story so far would be bad--but not as bad as this! Somehow yesterday, when I started writing the above, I just felt positively ill. I even went to the bathroom to throw up, although it didn't come. Thinking about Mom and her story was what did it, of course. And having to write about it somehow makes it that much worse.

I've come up with a new way to destroy this journal. I think I'll soak it overnight in water. Then when it's good and soggy and pulpy, I'll put it down the disposal where it will be shredded to--

Shredded. No, I won't do that after all. I can't shred Jonathon again. I've already done it once. After all, this journal IS Jonathon now, at least in a bizarre sort of way. I can't destroy it. Why do I keep thinking I want to destroy it? I've already destroyed him once! Why would I do it again?

Because this journal is NOT Jonathon. It's time to stop lying to myself. This is just a stinking journal in which I'm writing about all the awful decisions I've made and terrible things I've done. And the worst of all was what I did to Jonathon.

Oh, Jonathon! I'm so sorry! I never meant to do it! That is, not really! I didn't know what I was doing! I was just a stupid, mixed up kid who let herself be persuaded by others that an abortion was somehow ok. But it WASN'T ok, Jonathon. I know that now. It wasn't some simple procedure. It was a killing, pure and simple. Oh, Jonathon, I'm so sorry. I wish more than life itself that there was some way to make it up to you. But there's not, since you're dead. You're dead because of what I did. Because of me, you're gone forever.

My hand is trembling as I write this, so I hope my words turn out legible. What I learned that day from Doc Jenkins about Mom and her abortion was horrible. And everything I've been thinking and saying and writing about Jonathon in this journal is what Mom was thinking and saying about me. ME! Because when she went to the doctor that day for her abortion, she was pregnant with me. And a week later she came back and had the abortion performed to terminate me.

That's right. Mom did to me what I did to Jonathon. The very same thing. She struggled and cried about it beforehand like I did, but just like me, she went ahead and did it. And one of the biggest reasons she did was because the boy who got her pregnant--Dad as it turns out--was urging her to do it. Just like Bob, he kept telling her it was the only way, that she had no choice, that she had to do it. And just like me, she let herself be persuaded and did it. And just like me, she regretted it afterward with everything in her heart.

I'm getting off on a tangent again, aren't I? If anyone else was reading this now, they'd say, "You're nuts. What you've just said is impossible. If she'd had an abortion, you'd be dead. You wouldn't be writing this right now."

True enough. But she DID go through with her abortion, and she did agonize over it afterward. And then, three weeks after she'd had it done a miracle happened. But it's not the miracle you're probably thinking. It's not that her abortion was merely unsuccessful. Rather, it turned out that she hadn't actually had one at all!

Doc Jenkins told it best in his own words. All the while he was telling me this story I felt unreal, as if I was an observer watching a play unfold on a stage. But I also knew I was much more than an observer in this play. I was there. I was the baby. I was Jonathon.

"Carol happened to glance at the newspaper on this day, about three weeks after her abortion," said Doc Jenkins. "She was very depressed, and had turned to reading to try and keep her mind off what she had done to you, Kate. And she came across a very interesting article. An article that changed her life."

"It was about how a young doctor who had recently started working at an abortion clinic in town was having his medical license revoked. It seems this doctor had been engaged in a vast pretense. He was secretly very much against abortions, you see, and had concocted a plan to fight them in a small way. He applied to work at the abortion clinic and was accepted. He then 'performed' abortions on roughly a dozen women. But in reality, he had not aborted any of their babies. He only pretended to. He even succeeded at fooling the inexperienced nurse who assisted him, claiming that he was using a new procedure that she knew nothing about."

"He knew he would be found out eventually and stripped of his license. But he also knew how he felt about abortion, and decided that if he could save just one baby--just one, mind you--the sacrifice of his career would be worth it. His main hope was that if the mothers on whom he'd done the 'abortion' found out they had a second chance, they'd have a change of heart and keep their babies this time."

"And that is exactly what your mother did, Kate. She found to her inexpressible relief that her 'abortion' had not happened at all! You were still healthy and growing inside her all the time. And when she found this out she utterly refused to have a true abortion when the clinic offered her one for free, to make amends for the doctor's deception. More than half of the other dozen women on which he had performed his sham abortions decided like your mother, and also let their babies live. Unfortunately, however, a few of them went through with their second--and this time real--abortion."

At this point in his story, I just stared at Doc Jenkins in horror. The thought of Mom having an abortion was unthinkable. It was like eating a delicious piece of pie, only to find a roach in the last bite. In fact, it was worse than that. I found my breath coming in short gasps as if I had just been running a long distance. I nearly felt like I was hyperventilating!

I was an aborted baby! ME! I was supposed to have been killed, just like Jonathon! I was supposed to be dead! My mother and father had both decided to terminate me! The conflicting emotions that coursed through me at this knowledge was almost more than I could take. And I knew it was going to take my feeble brain a while to digest all this, and come to terms with hit. I knew I'd be thinking about this for a long time to come.

I had been saved by a miracle. Out of the hundreds of thousands of abortions that happen in this country every year, I was one of about a dozen babies supposedly 'aborted' by this doctor, that had a very unexpected second chance! And my Mom had taken that chance, bless her heart! Because if she hadn't, I wouldn't be here, writing this right now. I'd be dead. Stone dead.

I just couldn't get over it.

"The other women who had the second chance and saved their babies," continued Doc Jenkins, "were all greatly relieved, of course. But none were as relieved as your mother. The realization that she had aborted you weighed so heavily on her mind for those three intervening weeks that she reached a point of mental instability. The guilt was too much. The young doctor was not able to tell her and the others anything of course, since he wanted to discretely do as many sham 'abortions' as possible before being discovered. So for those three weeks, your mother was absolutely convinced that she had aborted you. You were dead to her, and her grief was inconsolable. Her mind was already starting to sink into oblivion when she found the article, and that saved her sanity just in time. If she had gone just a few more days, it would have been too late."

Doc Jenkins suddenly reached down to the candy plate Mom always kept on our coffee table and helped himself to a butterscotch. A funny little voice in my mind piped up, "How can he eat a butterscotch candy at a time like this, when he's just told me I should be dead!"

I looked down and was surprised to see that my hands were shaking. And then I suddenly blurted. "Thank you. Thank you, Doctor for saving my life. Because of you, I am alive today."

Doc Jenkins looked at me in surprise. "I have not revealed the identity of this doctor! What makes you think it was me?"

"But he is you!" I blurted. Somehow I know it is."

"Hogwash," was all he said casually, while sucking on his butterscotch. "You have no proof. At any rate, to continue the story, this poor doctor had a rough go of it afterward. It took five years before he could get his license back again, during which time he worked at a car wash. And he has been so frowned on by his colleagues even to this day that he cannot lease any space in any doctor building in town. Therefore, he must offer his services out of his own home."

"But that's you!" I cried again. "You work out of your own home!"

He merely shrugged. "So do many doctors. But enough of such wild speculations. Your mother is the point of our discussion today, not some unknown doctor. I'm afraid that even though she found out you were still alive, her mind did not fully grasp that reality at first. For much of the time she seemed perfectly normal. But at other times she would unaccountably start to cry and carry on because she had aborted her baby. I must say that your father showed his true colors at this point. Instead of urging her to have a second abortion, he begged her forgiveness and urged her to have the baby, promising that he would marry her and support her. He was the main one who was instrumental in restoring her to mental health, by constantly and gently reassuring her that her 'little Katydid' as she called you was indeed still alive, and would soon be born. She was always certain you would be a girl, and knew that she would call you Kate."

Just like I always knew that Jonathon would be Jonathon. The joy of finding I had been spared from abortion death was stopped short by the memory of what I had done to Jonathon. If only the doctor had done his deception two weeks ago at the clinic I went to, rather than 19 years ago! But if he had, I would never have been born 19 years ago!

A wild and completely illogical hope suddenly jumped into my fevered brain. "What about my abortion?" I cried. "Was it real? Or was it a fake, like the one Mom had?"

Doc Jenkins shook his head sadly. "I took the liberty of having a friend of mine inquire at the abortion clinic where yours was performed, as soon as I heard you'd had yours done there. I was sure that question would come up, either from you or from Carol. But I'm afraid lightning has not struck twice in the same place this time. Your abortion was legitimate, and was properly performed."

At my crestfallen look he reached over and patted my hand gently. "I don't judge you, Kate. I never judge the mother in these cases. She has enough of a burden to carry without feeling like everyone around her is judging her. But now you suddenly have another life in your hands. Your mother needs you, Kate. I'm afraid when she learned about your abortion, it triggered her repressed memories of the terrors she went through for those three weeks before she found out the truth. I was hoping when I took you upstairs a few minutes ago that the sight of you--a fully grown, mature Kate, the girl she raised for 18 years--would restore her mind, at least somewhat. But you saw what happened." He sighed. "I'm afraid her condition is more serious than I'd thought."

"Will she recover?" I asked, a dim sense of terror gripping my heart. The thought of Mom never being Mom again was more than I could take.

"I don't know," he responded. "Perhaps a specialist could answer that question, and I've already urged your father to retain one immediately. But I firmly believe you can help her regain her health by simply being here for her, going in to see her often, reassuring her that you ARE Kate, no matter what she says or how much she denies it. Like your father did 19 years ago, you can help her gain her life back."

I shook my head. "But won't the sight of me just make her problem worse? After all, it was finding out I'd had an abortion that triggered this!"

Doc Jenkins sighed again. "True enough," he said. "But her main problem is not your abortion but her own. While she's going to have to accept the reality of your abortion someday, in the meantime just seeing you every day should trigger her memories of you as the girl she raised, and help her to recover. In other words, I'm convinced your presence will do her more good than harm. And she needs you desperately. Of course, it will be best if you don't discuss or mention your abortion around her. Just focus on helping her remember that she did NOT abort you. You'll do all you can to help her, won't you?" There was an intense pleading in his eyes.

"Of course," I responded automatically. And I instantly knew part of the reason for the intensity of his gaze. I'm no dummy, and knew his urging me to do this wasn't just to help Mom. Part of it was obviously intended to help ME to recover from my own abortion, by having someone to serve and help and get my mind off my own problems. Doc Jenkins was a pretty sharp guy.

"You've got a lot of your father in you," he said with a slight smile. "A lot of that old fire and strength of his. I think things will turn out all right for you all."

As if on cue, Dad suddenly came in the door. He gazed at me with an odd pleading in his eyes, knowing that the awful story and his part in it had been told.

Before I could say a word, he blurted, "Please forgive me Kate. I hope you won't judge me too harshly. I was wrong, and have regretted it ever since. I cannot imagine life without you. I've been unspeakably grateful ever since Doc Jenkins did what he did."

"So, you WERE the doctor in the story!" I said to Doc Jenkins accusingly. He just grinned in a goofy, embarrassed way. But I didn't say this just to accuse him. Actually I did it to divert attention from the intensity of Dad's gaze, and the agony in his eyes. It almost seemed he was on the verge of tears again, which was so foreign to his normal personality that I hardly knew what to say or do. I wasn't sure I could handle it if he lost his composure again.

But my little diversion tactic didn't work. Dad was still looking at me with an intensity that obviously would not go away. And suddenly I melted and rose from my chair and he was hugging me once again.

"Oh, Daddy, of course I forgive you! I love you! I know you would never do anything to hurt me. That was just a mistake you made, long ago." I could feel water on my shoulder again as he started balling. And suddenly my own floodgates opened once more and another deluge took place. And while Doc Jenkins stood awkwardly by looking on, I found myself wishing with all my heart that it was Jonathon I was hugging, not Dad, and that HE was the one that had said those words to me.

Oh, how I wished to hear those words from him! How I yearned to hear his little voice say, "I forgive you! I forgive you!"

But he was dead, and could not say them.

MAY 4

In the midst of all the drama and trauma, I found out when I went to bed that night that Oscar had run away. Apparently when I stayed at Clarice's house the night before and didn't come home, he decided he had to go out and find me and bring me back. I was devastated, of course. On top of everything else, losing him was almost too much. But thankfully he came wandering back two days later, looking fatter if anything, and very contented with himself. I don't know where he went, but it must have been a good place. I was just grateful that he had not died and left me too, which would have been yet another death I caused.

The next month was one of the most difficult of my life. Every night I had my dreams of Jonathon. Sometimes they haunted me so much, I could hardly sleep. Always he was there, staring at me with those horrible, adoring baby-eyes. A few nights I woke up screaming. Only this time, mom didn't come in to comfort me as she had before.

My days were haunted too, in a way. Dad was wonderful and so was Doc Jenkins, but Mom was not good at all. She just lay there, getting thinner and thinner, and refused to recognize me. I would go in and sit with her for hours, talking with her as if everything was normal. I would bring up things we had done together in the past and places we'd been. I even confessed a few of my misdeeds from childhood days that she'd never known about, like the time I put her favorite curling iron down the toilet. But she would just stare at me with her big, limpid eyes, and say nothing. The few times she would talk, it was simply to say that Kate was dead, because she had killed her. This did not help me of course, and made me feel even greater guilt about Jonathon.

It was obvious to me that not only had I killed my baby, I had basically killed my mother as well. Doc Jenkins kept insisting I was doing good with my efforts every day, and so did the specialist Dad brought in to look at her. But I remained unconvinced.

And why should I think any differently? The baby that had so miraculously been returned to her had turned around and betrayed her! In a way, the Kate she had so lovingly raised HAD died, and was no more. That Kate died the day she killed her own baby, Jonathon. So in a way mom was right when she said her Kate was dead. The Kate everyone saw now was just a shell that was walking around, going through the motions day by day. It was not the same person at all.

I dropped out of school. It was a stupid thing to do I know, but with Clarice gone and after my falling out with Bob, I just couldn't face the whole school scene again. School didn't have any meaning anymore. As for Clarice, I kept trying on Facebook and gmail to reach her, but she never responded. I frequently went back to her house to see if she or her Mom or Dad had returned, but there was never anyone there. I had no idea how her Dad could stay away from his job that long. But one day as I drove by, I was surprised and discouraged to see a 'For Sale' sign out front. When I called the realtor about it, all she said was that the owner lived in Florida.

As for Bob, he called me again after about two weeks. Because of my Mom and Dad's story in which Dad had such a huge change of heart, I decided to answer his call and talk to him. It wasn't out of any interest I had in him, since he no longer meant anything to me. I just wanted to see if he would react the same way Dad did.

"Gee, it sure is great to her your voice," he said ecstatically.

"It's good to hear yours too," I lied. My heart struggled briefly with the memory of the cute, ruggedness that had initially attracted me to him. But the struggle was very brief. All I had to do was remember what he'd said in his house that day, and the feeling left immediately.

"So, what's been happening?" he asked. "I haven't seen you at school."

"I decided to finish high school online," I lied. "It's quicker that way." That was a total crock of course, since I had been too depressed to work on any classes. My carefully created high school GPA was in a shambles--but I didn't even care. I simply didn't care about things like that anymore.

"Senior sluff day is next week," he said. "And after that's graduation."

I felt a slight twinge of regret--but only a very slight one. It was nothing like the regret I felt about killing Jonathon. "Are you going?" I asked.

"Sure," he answered. There was silence for a moment. We were both obviously trying very hard to avoid any mention of the punch in the nose or the abortion. But the truth was, I was just trying to give the impression all was normal again, to get his guard down so I could spring my question.

"So," he said in that casual way that told me he was about to make a proposition, "how about if we get together? Maybe this Friday? We could do pizza and a movie."

It sounded like he might be sufficiently lulled into a false sense of normalness. I decided to spring my trap. "Gee I'd love to," I said, "but on Friday Dad and I are going to go out crib shopping for the baby."

I heard a strangled, choking sound on the other end of the line. "What did you say?" he blurted in a husky voice.

"You know," I said, trying to act casual. "The baby. OUR baby. The one that you're the father of. Isn't it wonderful that the abortion wasn't successful, and that he'll be born soon?"

The phone suddenly went dead. And when he didn't call back as the days and weeks passed, I had my answer. Bob was NOT like my Dad. Not at all. But the saddest part was that my lie about crib shopping wasn't true. The abortion had not failed, and Jonathon was indeed dead. Dad and I would not be going crib shopping for Jonathon, now or ever.

One day a few weeks later, I sent a text at random to Bob's Mom saying her son had got me pregnant, then convinced me to have an abortion. It was my parting shot, to make his

life interesting.   Unfortunately, I never got a
response.

MAY 12

It's been a few days since I've written in this disgusting journal. I decided at the last minute to postpone my therapy appointment, mainly because I hadn't got my story in here finished and I knew he'd ask about it. Then when I finally did meet with him even though I hadn't finished, he surprised me by saying he was pleased I was still writing in this silly thing since a lot of his patients either throw their journals down the sewer or put catsup on them and microwave them. This made me think there must be some psychological connection between all of his patients, since those are two things I've been sorely tempted to do more than once. One of these days I just might, too.

Anyway, he said to keep writing in here but that I could take my time, since he said the most important thing is to simply write every day. "You must learn to harvest the energy of time!" he said dramatically, using one of the trite sayings he likes to use. "Do a little tidbit of something big every day, and one day you'll wake up and realize you've done far more than you ever expected! And THAT is harvesting the energy of time."

I think he's nuts. But I guess I must be nuts too since I keep going to see him. Anyway, I'll put his 'energy of time' idea to use and keep going with my lousy story.

Time passed. Soon it was summer and three months had gone by since I'd killed my baby. The dreams still haunted me almost every night. Mom still refused to respond, and simply lay limp in her bed all day. I still felt constant guilt about what I'd done and the lives I'd ruined.

But in spite of all that, my life seemed to be returning to something that could maybe be called 'normal.' It was not a return to the way life had been before of course, since that was impossible. That previous 'me' was dead, having truly died the day I killed Jonathon. But I was getting used to my routine of dragging myself through each day. I was still to freaked out over what I'd done to go to school or work, so my job was to watched over mom while dad went to work every day. I tried to be cheerful and talkative around her, although she never seemed to respond to my efforts. I also tried to cheer up Dad in the evenings too, when he got depressed about how Mom wasn't progressing. On top of these challenges, I still had to just cope with the awful things I'd done, and with the never ending knowledge that I'd killed Jonathon. Life was not very pleasant at all.

But yes, something called 'normalcy' had finally come back to my life. However, one day something happened that shattered it like glass.

It was Clarice. I drove by her house like I often did, just to see if the 'For Sale' sign was still there, and if there was any evidence of people inside. I never expected any change, of course. But this time, to my surprise, the sign was indeed gone, and I could see lights on inside since it was dusk. Excitedly I pulled over to the curb and got out. Obviously someone had bought the home and moved in, so there was no sense in my going to the door. After all, never in a million years would Clarice be home like she used to be in the olden days. That was all a long ago dream. There was someone new living here now. I kept telling myself these things as I went to the door, trying to prepare myself so I wouldn't be disappointed when she didn't answer.

But that crazy side of me that had to have things PROVEN to it had taken over. I rang the bell and waited, my heart pounding. "She won't be here, you dope," I kept telling myself. But my heart kept racing just the same.

The door opened and to my shock Clarice was indeed standing there. I simply could not believe it!

But that's not the only shock I received. Indeed, it was at this instant that my world totally shattered. Her belly was big! She was going to have a baby!

"Clarice!" I said stupidly, staring not at her face but at her belly.

"Kate!" she answered just as stupidly, in a voice that sounded almost frightened.

That was all either of us said for a moment. It was the most awkward moment we had ever shared together.

"So," I said, trying to sound casual. "When did you get back in town?"

"Uhm, just yesterday," she answered, in a strained voice that was also an attempt at being casual. "Our house sold, so we have to move stuff out. We live in Florida now."

"Really?" I said, as if I didn't already know.

There were sudden footsteps in the hall behind her. "Is someone at the door, Clarice?" called out her mother's voice.

"No Mom," answered Clarice loudly. "I just thought I'd go out and sit on the front porch for a minute."

"Ok," came the answer. "But don't stay out too long. The mosquitoes will eat you alive."

I stared at Clarice dumbly as she quickly came out and shut the door, then grabbed my hand. "Come here!" she said insistently, leading me over to the bench on her porch. "We need to talk."

"You just lied to your Mom," I said stupidly. "Why didn't you tell her I was here?"

"Because she doesn't want me to talk to you!" came her sharp answer. "Who do you think has kept me from contacting you all this time?"

"Don't give me that!" I suddenly cried. "You could have at least contacted me on Facebook if you'd wanted to! Your Mom couldn't have prevented it."

"She could if she made sure I didn't have access to a computer!" she hissed back at me. "Which I didn't!"

"You expect me to believe your Mom was holding you prisoner in Florida? That's crazy!"

Clarice suddenly hung her head and didn't say anything for a minute. Then she whispered, "Yeah, you're right I guess. That is crazy. I'm 18. I could have insisted on contacting you no matter how much she protested. But I didn't. I just couldn't. Not after what I did to you." I saw a tear fall. "I never thought I'd see you again."

A sudden wave of compassion swam over me, followed by a wave of confusion. "I don't get any of this. What's going on?"

Clarice looked up at me with glistening eyes. "Isn't it obvious?" she said. "I'm having a baby--a boy, according to a recent ultrasound. I'm having the baby I told you I was going to abort. Remember how I called you a few days before I was going to the abortion clinic? Your voice sounded so sad and miserable, I suddenly knew I couldn't go through with it and do what you did. And so I betrayed you. I told you to get an abortion and that it was perfectly all right to do so. But when it came down to it, I couldn't do it myself."

"You mean the sadness in my voice stopped you?" I asked in surprise. Part of me was greatly relieved to think that I'd saved my best friend from the agony I'd been going through--just by having a sad voice!

She smiled weakly. "Not just that. I got to thinking about it too. And I realized it's all right for people to say 'a woman has a choice' and even to urge an abortion when it's not your own baby you're talking about. But this was MY baby! And I just couldn't do it. I couldn't, Kate. I love my little Michael! I couldn't do that to him! So I confessed everything to my mother-- but not to my dad of course, since he'd have blown his top. And she quickly arranged for us to just get away to Florida for awhile, and start a new life and ... and ... " Her voice trailed off.

A lump had come up in my throat that threatened to cut off my oxygen supply. "Michael?" I repeated dumbly.

She nodded her head. "Remember that silly game we used to play in fifth grade, about what we'd name our first baby boy when we had one? Michael was always my favorite. Just like yours was always Jonathon."

I choked suddenly, to hear someone else utter the name that for many months now I had only been saying in my own mind. "Jonathon," I repeated, the tears starting to glisten in my own eyes.

"Oh, Kate, please forgive me!" cried Clarice suddenly, throwing her arms around me. "I didn't mean to talk you into it. I didn't mean for you to kill your little Jonathon. I'm so sorry! I'm so sorry!" She then started blubbering, and was reduced to a mass of helpless tears.

Curiously however, I didn't join her. True, my eyes were glistening and threatening to unloose a storm of my own. But something held me back. Whether it was stubborn, cruel unforgiveness or just crabby obstinacy, I didn't know. Or maybe I was just becoming more hardened because I had killed my baby, and people who kill like me are hardened.

But when I looked at her big belly, I suddenly knew the reason I wasn't crying. It wasn't lack of forgiveness or harshness. It was just plain, old-fashioned jealousy. Jealousy that bordered on anger and hatred. She was having a baby. And I wasn't. And even though I was glad for her, I also felt anger toward her at the same time. It was stupid, I know, but that's what I felt.

I stood up abruptly. "I've got to go," I announced flatly. And I meant it to, in more ways than one. It was only too obvious that Clarice and I could never be friends again. She would always have Michael. He would be born and grow up with her, and become a day-to-day part of her life. I could never visit her or talk with her or have anything to do with her without Michael being part of it. And because of Jonathon, I knew that was not something I could live with.

"Oh, Kate," begged Clarice grabbing my hand, her face a mess of tears. "Please don't leave me like this! Please at least say you forgive me! Please! I can't bear it if you don't! You've always been the strong one between us. You've always been the one who could do things I was too weak to do. I can't go on if you don't say it, Kate! I can't!"

I looked at her in shock. ME, the strong one? I'd always thought the strong one between us was HER! I looked into her pleading eyes as they gushed out a river of tears. And I suddenly saw in those eyes, in spite of Michael, the same old Clarice I used to know. The same dear friend that had always meant so much to me. And then my heart melted and my own tears started to flow and we hugged each other and I found myself saying over and over, "I forgive you Clarice. I forgive you. I know you didn't mean to hurt me or Jonathon. I know you didn't. I forgive you."

We spent about ten minutes like that, gushing tears on her front porch like two moronic babies. Then suddenly her Mom came out and found us. And to my surprise, her eyes were cold and hard.

"Clarice needs to come in now, Kate," she said in a tight voice. "Say good-night please."

I looked at her curiously. So Kate hadn't been joking when she'd said her Mom didn't want her talking to me. But why the anger? Why keep us apart?

Yet even as I thought the question I knew the answer. I had had an abortion. Clarice had not. And unlike those mothers I'd seen with their daughters at the abortion clinic, abortion was something Clarice's Mom could ever go along with. And out of unreasonable fear that in some bizarre way I might talk Clarice into it--like she had talked ME into it--I was a threat to her daughter that had to be put aside!

I felt a sudden, unaccountable gush of love for Clarice's Mom in spite of the way she was glaring at me. Here was a woman who would never support an abortion, no matter what personal embarrassment or trouble might follow! Hallelujah! If only there were more women and mothers like her.

"Good night, Clarice," I said, giving her hand a squeeze. She just looked at me guiltily, trying to excuse her Mom with her eyes. "It's all right, Clarice. Maybe after Michael is born, you can send me a picture."

Clarice's Mom looked at me in surprise. "Good night," I said as I passed where she was standing by the door. "And thanks for letting me stay at your house." She gazed at me in a confused way, but I offered no further explanation.

I knew as I walked away that would be the last time I would ever see Clarice or her mother.

If she ever sent me a picture of Michael, I would throw away her letter without opening it. There was NO way I would ever be able to look at a picture of her baby. And there was simply no way I could maintain any contact with her in light of all that had happened.

So I had caused another death. The death of a friendship that at one time Clarice and I thought would never end.

I was happy for her of course. Happy for her for making the choice I should have made. Happy that she had had enough sense to tell her Mom before going to the abortion clinic. Happy that she would have Michael and be able to enjoy him for the rest of her life. Happy that she didn't have to live with the daily agony of regret I lived with, wishing every day with all my heart that I'd done things differently, and that I hadn't killed Jonathon.

A sudden question leapt into my mind. If I'd told my Mom about my pregnancy before going to the abortion clinic, what would she have done? Would her mind have gone bad? Would she be in the condition she was now?

I shook my head as if to clear it from a fog. I wasn't exactly sure. But I had a very strong suspicion she would have handled it ok. After all, pregnancy is not the same thing as abortion. She would have been shocked to find out I was pregnant of course. But because of her own experience, there is NO WAY she would have urged me to have an abortion. Quite the opposite! If only I'd had the sense to tell her privately like Clarice told her mom, I never would have killed Jonathon and mom would not be a mental case today.

Indeed, from what I could tell, it was the past-tense reality of my having terminated my pregnancy with an abortion that had caused her mental problem. It had somehow triggered the horror she thought had been removed. Abortion was death. Pregnancy was life. If I'd told her, she would have done the same as Clarice's mom. I was sure of it.

I sat up on my bed a long time that night, thinking and rubbing Oscar as he purred contentedly. As always, Mom was just the same when I got home. Her condition had not changed, and she hadn't improved at all in the passing months. In fact, if I was honest with myself, she looked like she was getting worse. She seemed to be losing weight, and was talking less and less. She was obviously slipping away, and growing more and more distant.

A sudden wave of depression and hopelessness washed over me. What was I doing here, anyway? High school was over, Bob was out of my life, I had no friends, no job, and no hope for the future. I was too depressed to even consider going back to school or going to work anyway.

But that's not all. I had killed my baby and I had as good as killed my Mom, and now my best friend was going to have a baby because she wasn't an idiot like me who decided to kill it instead. I was a murderer! Just a common murderer! In my depressed condition the words started to repeat themselves over and over in my mind: "You're a murderer! You're a murderer! You're a murderer!"

And you know what they do to murderers.

MAY 14

It's funny how I'd begun to think I was coming to cope with my abortion, and that my life was starting to sort of be normal again--then suddenly I not only was back to square one but seemed even worse off. Things were bad in the beginning, but at least then I had Clarice, and Mom and even Bob to turn to. Now I had none of them. Dad was wonderful of course, but it was obvious Mom's condition was starting to wear him down. He was losing weight like she was, and was starting to get snappish and irritable at the slightest little things.

And the dreams of Jonathon had not decreased. It had been months now since I'd killed him, but the pain and guilt had not gone away like they were supposed to. If anything, they were getting worse. And the day I saw Clarice--and knew as I walked away that I would never see her again--was the day that it all just snapped. Somehow, the vague hope that Clarice would come back into my life again and in some indefinable way help me make sense of everything and find a purpose for living was now gone. I had no hope left. And there was nothing left for me to keep fighting for.

I decided to do it with my car. There was a very steep cliff not far outside of town, with only a light guard rail. If I hit the rail in the right spot at high speed I would be guaranteed to go over the edge. I could then join Jonathon and Dad would get a nice insurance settlement to help pay for all of Mom's medical bills that were piling up. As for Mom, she thought I was dead already anyway. Dad would be upset of course, but he was strong, like Doc Jenkins said. And in truth, he was the only one that would miss me.

Not having any reason to wait, I put my plan into action the very next morning. And wouldn't you know it, just like I bungle up most things, I bungled up my own death too. I was speeding to get there, just to get it over with-- and then I caused an accident! I sped through a red light and smacked into another car. The other driver wasn't hurt fortunately, but I was keenly disappointed that I also walked away without a scratch. Why was I cursed to live when I so much deserved and wanted to die? Unfortunately my car was totaled, so the cliff idea was out.

My accident shocked Dad out of his malaise somewhat, since he just about freaked out with worry when the police brought me home. "Kate! Are you sure you're all right?" he'd cried, bounding down the stairs and giving me a huge hug. At that point I almost felt a twinge of regret about my plan to kill myself, with his showing so much genuine concern about me.

But then suddenly, everything switched. He took a step back and started to frown, then proceeded to ball me out for speeding and being stupid and reckless. So I changed my mind. I knew what I had to do, and all I needed was a different way to do it. I had passed the sentence of death on myself for killing Jonathon, and I intended to carry out the execution.

Dad found me in the bathroom that night trying to slit my wrists. Unfortunately I'd chosen a rather dull kitchen knife and had not succeeded in drawing much blood--yet. Poor Dad went so white with fright I thought he might have a heart attack. Then he immediately called 911. Within 24 hours I found myself locked up in a safe house for attempted suicides like me, with my wrists wrapped up in bandages. My walls were padded, and I had nurses checking on me constantly to make sure I hadn't figured out a new way to kill myself.

"Why did you do it, Kate?" asked Dad in a tired voice when he visited me the next day. "You know your mother and I love you! Why would you want to hurt us like this?"

"Mom thinks I'm dead already," I responded mechanically. "And I wish I was too. Then I could be with Jonathon."

"Jonathon?" asked my Dad, raising an eyebrow. To my surprise, I suddenly realized I'd never told him the name of my baby that I'd killed. "He's my baby. Or rather, he was. I just want to go where he is."

"But Kate," said my Dad, running his hand through his hair in exasperation, "that's not the way these things work." He breathed out a long, low sigh. It was clear he was trying to find some way to reach me, and convince me that my worthless life was worth living. "Killing yourself isn't the answer, Kate. Killing is never the answer."

"I know. I found that out when I killed Jonathon."

"There, you see?" he responded, as if he'd suddenly said something profound. "You said it yourself--killing is not the answer, and another killing won't help anyone. You have to learn to cope instead. You have to learn to forgive, even when what you did seems unforgivable. Believe me, I know. I felt just like you once, like I'd been an accomplice to murder regarding your mother's abortion. And I considered the same avenue of escape."

"Really?" I asked in surprise. Dad had considered suicide? That was news.

"I nearly tried it too. But a wise friend talked me out of it. She convinced me that the power of forgiveness was the power of giving, not taking. When you forgive, you 'give for.' And the person you 'give for' most is YOU."

"I'm not worth it," I said blandly. "The only thing I want to give myself is a way out of this world."

"Look," he said gently. "Forgiveness of self is the most important kind of forgiveness there is. That's because we know ourselves much better than anyone else, and we know the many things we've done wrong. When we forgive ourselves we're saying, 'I may have done horrible things, but I forgive myself. Whether I deserve it or not, I forgive, because God forgives me and wants me to forgive myself.' And when you say that to yourself, you then let it go, knowing that you would never do it again in a million years. And by doing that you're GIVING something--a gift to yourself of having a second chance."

I looked at him with a blank expression on my face.

"I don't want to get all preachy on you," he continued. "But that's precisely why Jesus came to earth. He didn't come here for himself, since he was already perfect. He came to help us--all of us. He knew we would make mistakes, and that sometimes they would be terrible mistakes that we would think we simply could not forgive ourselves for. But HE made it clear that he would forgive us regardless. And then he took on himself the pain that all of our terrible mistakes ever caused. He experienced every bit of that agony. He knows the pain you're feeling Kate, because he's felt it himself! He felt it for you! You don't have to pay the price of total anguish for that sin of abortion, because he already did. All you have to do is ask God in true remorse to forgive you, and to apply the blood of Christ to make you clean--and then you can be clean and free of it. But that can't happen if you don't forgive yourself. When you hold back on forgiveness of yourself, you're basically saying God is a fool to forgive you, and you know better than Him whether you are worthy of it. And it's never wise to call God a fool."

I stared at my Dad, dumfounded. I'd never heard him talk like this. We went to church, but I'd never heard him say much about the stuff they said there. Now he was talking about all this as if he knew it from personal experience. Which, I had to admit, maybe he did.

"What you need is to forgive yourself, and give yourself a second chance," he repeated. "And then you need a focus. You need to put your energy and talent into some worthy goal so you can stop dwelling on the abortion."

"A focus?" I said dumbly. "Like what?" I couldn't think of any worthy goals to focus on, except maybe to kill myself.

"Anything that's good!" he said in exasperation. "It can be school or work or helping someone or service, or anything. Any goal that is bigger than you, that makes you feel like you're doing something that makes a difference, that contributes something to the world and leaves it a better place at least in some small way."

"I have nothing to contribute," I said dully.

"That's simply not true," countered Dad. "Everyone has something to contribute, no matter who they are, and no matter what they've done in the past or how untalented they may think they are. And I know you, Kate, well enough to know that you have many, many talents that can help lots of people--IF you'll just overcome your fixation on YOU long enough to do so."

"Fixation on me?" I blurted.

"Exactly," he said. "You're still in abortion mentality--thinking only of self. You feel hurt and guilty, and think you deserve to be punished. All of this is still just thinking of YOU. Do you honestly think if Jonathon were here right now, he would want you to kill yourself? Would that make HIM happy? Would it accomplish anything? Wouldn't he rather see you go out and do something to help someone else instead?"

This thought startled me. What would Jonathon think? Indeed, why had I never thought of that before? Yes, I'd killed him, but did that mean he wanted me to torture myself about it for the rest of my life? Would self-torture ever get me anywhere?

"You learned from your mistake," said Dad. "You know for yourself now, by personal experience, that abortion is a bad thing. You'll never do it again, right?"

I shook my head emphatically. Boy, did he have that right!

"Then it's time for you to move on," he said. "Sure, you'll still feel bad about it and feel regret at times--but you've got to stop dwelling on it, and try to fill your life with service and something positive to fill the void. Otherwise you'll go crazy."

I just stared at him, long and hard. This was pretty deep stuff, that I never thought my Dad was even capable of saying. But I couldn't deny a lot of it made sense. I thought I'd had a good goal in killing myself. But would another killing do anybody any good? Wouldn't it be better to do something productive instead? Wasn't living more helpful to others than dying?

These were pretty deep ideas that I'd have to mull over and think about for awhile. And from the look of this suicide house, it appeared that I'd have plenty of time here to do just that.

But one thing I knew for sure. If I did decide to change my goal of self destruction and pick a crusade to start fighting for, I had absolutely no doubt what that crusade would be. No doubt at all.

I would fight with all my power to end abortions.

MAY 17

Well, I'm back to writing in this stinking journal again. If anyone was to ever read this they'd see what a stupid dunce I've been. Killing Jonathon, driving my mom to the brink, then trying to murder myself. It's like I couldn't get enough of killing once I got started, even though I hated every minute of it.

I thought about what my Dad had said for a long time. That's not unusual really, considering where I was. After all, there was nothing else to do but sit there and think. Other than a doctor coming to check how my wrists were healing, and an occasional nurse checking to see that I wasn't trying to drown myself in a cup of water, I didn't have any other visitors. There was a TV, but I didn't feel like watching it. So I just sat there and thought.

Part of me hated to admit it, but a lot of what Dad said made sense. It wasn't logical that one killing justified another. Just because I killed Jonathon that didn't justify my killing someone else. Of course, that argument seemed a little shaky when I considered that the person I was trying to kill was just worthless me. That shouldn't count, after all. Who would care anyway, if I kicked the bucket? Only my Dad. It wasn't really killing, was it, if you were just snuffing out a worthless life?

Would Jonathon care? What would he think of it? I knew the question was crazy of course, since he was dead anyway. But if he was up in heaven looking down on me, what would he be thinking? Would he want me to kill myself as punishment for having killed him? Would that make him happy? Somehow that image didn't seem quite right. I just could not imagine Jonathon grinning in glee as he watched in heaven while I bled to death and died.

So, what would he feel? What would he want me to do? What advice would this innocent little person that I had so carelessly killed have to give to me, his murderer? The thought was disturbing. I didn't know the answer. All I knew was that I could not imagine him being happy if I killed myself.

I needed answers, but I wasn't getting any by just sitting and thinking. So I asked a nurse for a Bible to read. After all, Dad had talked about how Jesus suffered for me and all mankind, and he'd talked about how forgiving God was. I wasn't quite sure he had it right. I'd always thought God was stern and almost mean, and he didn't mind if one of his children who was wicked got what he deserved. Was he really that forgiving?

The Bible the nurse brought me was the opening of a new life for me. I quickly started reading and was instantly amazed. I just couldn't get over this man Jesus. Although I'd heard stories about him all my life at church, it was as if I was discovering him for the very first time. And what a remarkable person he was!

For example, instead of pursuing pleasure or money or a college degree or any of the other stupid things that I and everyone else are always going after, he just went around helping people.

He was as poor as dirt but he didn't care. All he seemed to care about was helping people. If he saw someone hurting, he tried to help them. That amazed me. Why would he do that? What did he get out of it? Most of the people he helped either didn't do what he told them afterward, or were just plain ungrateful. Like the people he told to keep his miracles quiet-- they usually went blabbing it all over town! And when he healed ten dudes who had a disgusting skin disease, only one of them bothered to thank him.

I found myself wondering as I read if I wasn't just being put on. Surely nobody could be THAT good. Nobody I'd ever met was that good. But whether I wondered or doubted or not, one thing was for sure. I WANTED it to be true. I wanted to believe there was someone out there like that who cared so much for others, and for me. Somehow it made me feel better to think there are people like that.

And then in one of those rare moments when my feeble brain actually has an insight, I realized one day that there ARE people like that out there. Dad was one. So was Mom, at least before she lost her mind because of what I did to her. Clarice's Mom was like that too. These were people who loved someone else so much, they would do almost anything for them, even if it caused them pain or death.

And then suddenly I felt just that much worse. These examples were all parents! The people they cared about were their children! Why was I such a disgusting worm of a person that I killed my child instead of caring for them like all these other parents?

I threw my Bible in the corner when that realization came to me. Then I finally turned on the TV and started watching mindless game shows, and pointless competitions where they always try to make it sound like winning the competition is so important it's like life or death. That's complete garbage of course, but the people on those shows do a pretty good job of acting when they get all worked up over nothing.

The Bible sitting in the corner started gnawing at me. It just sat there taunting me, making me wish I could throw it out the window and get it out of my sight. But of course my windows were locked, since they didn't want me to jump out one of them. I decided to ask the nurse to take the Bible away.

But when she came in to make sure I wasn't trying to stand on my head in an effort to pass out, I found myself thanking her for the Bible instead. What weirdness was this? Why was my mouth refusing to do what my brain told it to?

After that I went back to reading the Bible, but this time for a different reason. It was no longer to see if God was forgiving, but to look for evidence that it was all a big hoax. And that's precisely when God's forgiveness started jumping out at me from all the pages. And before long I forgot to look for hoax evidence at all.

The one that really hit me was the woman taken in adultery. I could identify with her, since I'd done the same thing. She was a despicable person, and the people who brought her to Jesus were right in demanding that she be punished. Being killed on the spot seemed a little extreme of course, but most probably she was the type of person who would have had an abortion if she could, so maybe it was justified.

Jesus' reaction to her blew me away. First he tells everyone there to go ahead and kill her if they felt they were sinless enough to do the job. They all felt guilty and left while he wrote in the dirt with his finger. He was obviously giving them a chance to leave without embarrassment. When he finally looked up, she was the only there. "Where are those thine accusers" he asked her in that strange Bible language they used back then for some reason. "Doth no man condemn thee?"

"No man, Lord," she answered, probably surprised to still be alive. She knew she was worthy of death, and maybe felt she deserved it to. Just like me.

"Neither do I condemn thee," said Jesus. "Go thy way and sin no more."

I started balling at that point. I just couldn't help it. Why would he forgive her? What good would it do? She DESERVED at least some punishment after all, for what she had done. Especially since, if what my Dad had said was right, Jesus KNEW he would be suffering later on for her awful sin, feeling the agony of it the same way she felt it. Why did he just forgive her and let her go?

I couldn't really figure it out. All I knew was that he did. All he wanted was for her to not do it again, and it was only too obvious she wouldn't. Neither would I, of course. No way would I ever have an abortion again. I didn't know how the "Dearie" lady and Dorothy Malk could have more than one. I never could.

The fact that Jesus forgave this woman made me feel good somehow. She was worthless, and so was I. If he could forgive her, maybe he could forgive me too.

But I couldn't forgive me. Even if God forgave, I could not. What I had done was just too despicable. How could I forgive such a horrible deed? Wouldn't that be the same as saying it was all right?

No, not quite. When Jesus forgave that adultery woman, he didn't say it was all right. He said the opposite by telling her not to do it again. He knew how bad it was, but he still forgave. How could he do that?

Every night I continued having the same dreams about Jonathon. He was always there, just watching me. After awhile I began to think maybe he was just waiting for me to pick up the abortion knives in some of my dreams and use them on myself instead of him. As soon as I got the idea, I tried it too. But it didn't work. Instead of causing me agonizing pain, any knife I used just disappeared the instant it touched me. That's the way it always is in a dream. And then I'd look up and Jonathon would still be looking at me. And it seemed at times that he had a tiny little tear in his eyes.

I kept reading the Bible. I'd become fascinated by the stories about this Jesus person who seemed to live at such a higher level than everyone else around him. I was amazed that he never spouted off at all the nonsense and stupidity he saw all the time in other people. The only people he spoke bad about were hypocrites, the people who thought they were doing everything right but really weren't. And even then he mainly said things that would help them realize their stupidity if they would only listen. He was obviously hoping they'd realize what lousy hypocrites they were and do something to change it.

It was his death on the cross that really got to me. There he was dying in agony, and suddenly for no good reason he suddenly said, "Father forgive them, for they know not what they do." I balled again when I read that. He was talking about the soldiers who killed him of course, pointing out that they were just fulfilling their orders and didn't know they were killing their God.

And then the thought came: Did I know what I had done when I had my abortion? Did I act knowingly? The answer was obvious--of course I did! I knew I was killing Jonathon! I'd done it knowingly, unlike those soldiers. I'd never felt quite right about it before I did it, but I did it anyway. I didn't deserve forgiveness like those soldiers did.

But then a little voice came into my mind. "Did you really know?" it asked. "If you had known you would be stopping its heart--if you had known the awful things Dorothy Malk said, would you have done it?" I knew instantly the answer was no. I definitely would not have done it if I had known. So did I really know what I was doing?

I could never really answer that question. In a way I did know, and in a way I didn't. I suppose I more did than didn't. But a part of me desperately wanted to believe I was at least partly innocent, that I'd been tricked by what people said and by the fact it was legal and supposed to be a 'woman's right.'

And then an even more startling thought came to me. The woman who committed adultery knew what she was doing, but Jesus still forgave her. It was amazing and impossible for him to do this of course, but he still did it. So even if I DID know what I was doing, he still wanted to forgive me. So maybe the question of whether I killed Jonathon knowingly didn't make any difference to forgiveness at all. All that mattered was to forgive.

That night was the first time in a long time I prayed. And in a way, it was my first real prayer ever, since all the prayers I'd ever said before were just spouted off without thinking. This time I prayed with real intent. I had a purpose. It was a simple prayer, really. All I said was, "God, thank you for Jesus. Thank you for how kind and forgiving he was. I wish he was here now. He would know what to do to help me. He always seemed to know what to say to people who were hurting and in pain, like I am."

That night I had another dream. It wasn't like the others. In this dream I was at the abortion clinic. But this time, instead of being the awful mother who was about to kill her child, somehow I knew I was the baby. Somehow I knew that terrible suction machine that would shred me to pieces was about to end my life. I cried out in fear and tried to cover my face with my eyes. But when I took my hands away, the clinic was gone and I found myself looking at Mom, lying in bed at home. Jonathon was floating in the air above her. "Kate's gone," I heard Mom say again, like she'd said so many times over the last few months while I sat next to her. "I killed her."

And then I totally lost control. "Kate's not gone!" I screamed at her. "I'm still right here! I didn't die! Don't you understand! I should have died--I wish I had--but I didn't. It's not your fault. It's not! It's not! I forgive you! I know you didn't really mean it! But even if you had, I forgive you! I forgive you!"

And then I was crying and sobbing all over again. And when you cry in a dream, unlike anything else you do in a dream, it seems to happen in the real world too. I know, because I woke up with my head plastered to a soggy pillow, and I was still balling my eyes out.

And then I understood. The question I'd had before was suddenly answered. I forgave my Mom. Even though she thought she'd done it-- even if she HAD done it knowingly--I forgave her. I saw how miserable she was. I didn't want her to be miserable like that. Maybe she'd made a wrong choice, but I didn't want her to suffer forever for it. I loved her and didn't want her to feel that way. That's why Jesus is so forgiving. He does it out of love, since it hurts him to see the ones he loves suffering and miserable. He wants them to put it behind them, and get on with life.

And now I also knew that Jonathon forgave me too, just like I forgave my mom.

MAY 20

I spent the rest of the night pacing across my little room and crying and beating my pillow and yelling at myself. The nurses must have thought it was normal behavior for someone in my condition, because none of them came in to see what was wrong. They just looked in the little window in my door to make sure I wasn't lying limp and dead on the floor.

I knew what I had to do now, but I didn't want to do it. I knew I had to forgive myself. If God and Jesus could forgive me, and if Jonathon could forgive me, then I needed to forgive me too.

But the trouble was, I didn't want to. I wanted to punish myself some more for what I had done. Somehow, it wasn't enough that I got to live while Jonathon was dead, and I could just waltz away and forgive myself and all would be well. A more severe punishment was certainly needed, and it was my duty to make sure it happened.

"Neither do I condemn thee. Go thy way, and sin no more." The words popped into my addled head unbidden. There was no further punishment in those words. Just forgiveness.

"Blast it all!" I yelled at the top of my wimpy lungs. "I know better! You're wrong, Jesus! I DO need to be condemned! I need to suffer! You're wrong! You're wrong!"

I knew how nonsensical it was to say that, of course. How could a perfect being be wrong? It was utterly impossible. And the ridiculousness of what I was saying overpowered me. By refusing to forgive, I was proclaiming that I was right and God was wrong! I was shouting to the world that I was smarter than God, and that God was a fool for being forgiving.

And like my Dad said, it's never wise to call God a fool.

I suddenly dropped to my knees and started sobbing over and over, "God forgive me! God forgive me! God forgive! I am SO sorry for what I did!" I continued like that for some time, wailing and twitching like I'd gone mad while continuing to repeat the same words. I wasn't sure I could forgive myself just yet, but I needed to ask God to forgive me. I knew he'd do it too, from the scriptures I'd read. But I needed to ask anyway.

Then suddenly another one of those dratted scriptures I'd read suddenly popped into my head. "For if ye forgive not men their trespasses, neither will God forgive your trespasses." His forgiveness depended on mine! He could not fully forgive me until I forgave myself! Until I did, my own determination to be punished blocked out his forgiveness. So I had to do it. I had to forgive the most unforgivable, disgusting, worthless person I'd ever known. I had to forgive ME.

I had never known self forgiveness would be so hard. What an agony. I beat my head on the padded wall. I slammed my fist painfully into my palm. I started swearing a blue streak, using every foul word I'd ever heard. If my mother had been there (before she lost her mind) she would have fainted. But I still knew I had to forgive myself. I had to do it.

I was fighting a phantom. I was fighting no one other than myself. I loathed myself, yet I was expected to forgive myself. I just couldn't do it! I just couldn't! Not after what I'd done to Jonathon.

The image of my dream came back into my mind. I heard myself yelling to my Mom once again. "I forgive you! I know you didn't really mean it! But even if you had, I forgive you! I forgive you!" And I knew Jonathon felt the same way. If even the murdered Jonathon could forgive me, why could I not forgive myself? If even Jesus could forgive me although he had to suffer all the tremendous pain for what I had done, why couldn't I forgive myself?

It went on like that for hours. I bashed my head against the padded wall so many times I was starting to get dizzy. I bit my hand, leaving a mark. I yanked on my hair until I'd pulled some of it out. But I knew that no matter what stupid, childish thing like that I did, I still had to face up and forgive myself.

And so, I finally did. Or rather, I tried. I just slumped on the floor and started saying over and over, "I forgive myself. I forgive myself. I forgive myself." It did no good at all, and the reason was obvious. I didn't mean a word of it. It took more than just words. It had to come from my heart. This was not something I could pretend away. I could not be a hypocrite and spout a few syllables and have all be well. I had to mean it with all my soul. And until I did mean it, the suffering would continue, even if it went on for years and years.

And then I realized with a start that by not forgiving I was making what Jesus suffered even worse. I was adding to his pain, by adding the pain of unforgiveness. My lack of forgiveness was a new evil that just caused more hurt. By refusing to forgive ME, I was making an already horrible sin even worse.

Sometime toward morning, it happened. At some undefined moment I finally opened up my heart and gave myself a second chance. I finally acknowledged that I'd done bad--really bad--but was forgiving myself for it anyway. And this time, I really meant it. I meant it with all my heart and soul.

And I kept repeating it over and over and over. "I forgive myself. I forgive myself. I forgive myself." Only this time, I meant what I was saying. And like a cool breeze takes the heat off a hot parking lot, the horror and loathing and anger and self-hatred I'd been feeling started to lift. It didn't happen instantly, but slowly it started to lift.

And then, because I was so exhausted from my all-night antics, I fell into a deep sleep. There was a smile on my face while I slept. Because in my dreams I once again saw Jonathon. Like always he was there, looking at me. But this time there was a difference. There were no abortion knives anywhere to be seen. For the first time I was not angry, or wracked with horrible guilt and self hatred. For the first time I did not yell for him to stop staring at me, or try to run away from him.

And for the very first time in any of my dreams, Jonathon smiled at me.

MAY 21

I thought my battle with forgiveness was over after that horrible night. I could not have been more wrong. Although I woke up with a more wonderful feeling of peace and happiness than I had felt in a very long time, by breakfast time things had somehow changed. The nurse brought me some pancakes and eggs, and the habitual thought that I regularly punished myself with every morning suddenly jumped unbidden into my mind. "I don't deserve to eat. I killed Jonathon." And in my heart I meant every word of it.

I yelled a profanity, startling the poor nurse. But in this place she was used to such behavior, and just smiled while she set the tray down. She even unwrapped my plastic fork and knife for me. Naturally I only got a flimsy plastic knife and fork with my food, since they couldn't let me have any metal.

I felt defeated. All that work last night, and the whole forgiveness thing just crashed down around my ears. I thought I'd forgiven myself! Why was I suddenly feeling the same old self-loathing that I usually felt? Was I such a loser that I couldn't even forgive right?

Then the dratted Bible got to me again. When Peter asked Jesus how often he should forgive and if seven times was enough, Jesus answered, "I say not unto thee, Until seven times: but, Until seventy times seven." That was 490 times for Pete's sake!

"Here I go again," I moaned, making the poor nurse look at me in pity as she left. I shoved my food tray aside and stood up so I could go and start the head bashing again. But before I reached the wall I tried saying, "I forgive me" as I had done last night. And although I really didn't mean it, I realized to my surprise, that I was not nearly as resistant to the idea as I used to be. Somehow I had broken the barrier last night in my first, and unquestionably worst, self-forgiveness session. And while it wasn't easy and my breakfast was long cold before I could finally say "I forgive myself" and truly mean it, I was thankfully able to gain back the hard won ground from the night before. I had to fight for it, but self-forgiveness finally came.

That was the start of a new life for me. For the first time since before I found out I was pregnant, I had hope. Hope is a precious thing, I realized. We can hardly live without it. If our lives are hopeless for too long, we start to slip into total despair and we lose our capacity to live. Sort of like Mom. Somehow she had lost all her hope.

But mine had returned. Because of Jesus it had returned. And even though I had to struggle many times a day to forgive myself-- almost every time I even thought about Jonathon and the abortion in fact--I was now able to forgive myself and start a new life. During those dark days after the abortion I had never thought I could reach such a point. But because of the Bible and Jesus and the incredible power of forgiveness, I did.

Days passed into weeks, and weeks into months. I was in that stinking place for almost three months. Dad came to see me every day of course. He didn't look too good some days. The double stress of caring for Mom and me trying to kill myself was almost too much for him. But after my forgiveness episode I started to improve and things got better. That helped Dad a lot. I started to be more positive and encouraging. I even laughed occasionally. It did my heart good to see him go away with a smile when he had come in with a haggard frown.

They were slow about letting me go. Apparently they were worried I might be putting on a show of improvement just so I could go drown myself in the river the minute I got out. But as the weeks passed and they saw that I consistently had a better attitude and was no longer anxious for a quick exit from the world, they finally got the message. They put me through a huge battery of psychological tests of course, just to make sure I was truly ready to re-enter the harsh world of reality. But I knew I was, and in time they came to see it to. And so finally in early October, they released me.

Dad was ecstatic while he drove me home, feeling tremendously relieved that one of his two burdens seem to have been lifted. "Kate, I can't tell you how good it is to see you out of that place. It's wonderful you're coming home."

I smiled at him weakly. It was strange, but I suddenly realized I didn't fully share his enthusiasm. I never thought I'd miss that awful suicide house, but being out after having been in such a protected environment felt a bit scary.

"Yeah, it is good," I said in as firm a voice as I could muster. Then just to change the subject I asked, "So how's Oscar?"

My Dad's face clouded over. "Uh ... Oscar ..." he repeated dumbly. He didn't need to say anything more.

"How long ago did he run away?" I asked quietly. Somehow the thought of not seeing his furry face when we got home was very depressing.

"Oh, awhile," he said vaguely.

"That long?" I said sadly. "Was it like the other time? Did he go trying to find me right after I disappeared?"

Dad nodded. "But he came back," he added hastily. "He left and came back several times."

"He expected me to be there when he came, I guess."

Dad nodded again. "I'm sure he'll come home again soon," he said with a forced smile. I almost asked how long it had been since the last time he came back, but then thought better of it. It was probably best that I didn't know.

"And how's Mom?" I asked, trying to change the subject again. Unfortunately, this wasn't a good subject to switch to. Dad's face clouded over once more.

"About the same," he answered vaguely. Then he reached over and gave me a reassuring pat on the arm. "But I'm sure she'll be much better when she sees you home again."

There was silence in the car for a few moments as we continued on our way home. Finally I brought up a plan that had been in my mind for quite awhile now. "I'm going to do a little research and find an anti-abortion demonstration group. I intend to join them and do all I can in the effort." There was a firm resolution in my voice. This was something I knew I HAD to do, for Jonathon and for me.

My Dad didn't know what to say to that. "That sounds good," he said at last. "But don't forget the GED. You need a high school diploma so you can move on with life, you know."

I knew that, but felt a bit overwhelmed and depressed by it too. I had missed graduation by just one semester because of the abortion. That blasted abortion had ruined about everything it could in my life.

We pulled into the driveway, and I found myself looking up at our house once more. It was the house I'd grown up in and which had been a constant refuge my whole life. It looked so familiar, yet at the same time sort of strange as if I didn't really belong here anymore.

The house wasn't different--I was. I had changed while it had stayed the same. And because of that, in some ways I had moved on. "I'm not returning to the way things were," I said firmly to myself in my mind. "I'm not going back. I can't. This is a new beginning, but in an old place."

Dad wasn't quite right when he said Mom was "about the same." She looked worse. When I first saw her, it scared me. Her face looked white and pinched and drained of blood, and her hands lay limply on the sheets. Her eyes had shrunken into her skull, and stared vacantly into the air in front of her.

"Look who's home, Carol," said Dad with forced cheerfulness. "It's Kate!"

Mom slowly looked at us, her eyes cloudy. "Kate?" she repeated stupidly. "But I killed Kate. She's not here."

"That's not true, Mom," I said firmly, stepping over and taking her hand. It felt like a cold, dead fish. "I'm right here."

She just stared at me without seeing. "Kate's gone," she said at last. "Gone forever because of what I did. She's gone."

I suddenly had a wild urge to shake her shoulders and yell in her face. I KNEW Mom was in the there somewhere, waiting to be pulled out. Why couldn't we reach her?

"I'm not gone, Mom," I repeated firmly. "I'm right here. I've come to take care of you, like you used to take care of me when I was a little girl." She continued to stare at me with unseeing eyes. And she didn't say anything for the rest of the evening.

MAY 23

True to my word, I found an anti-abortion group right away and called them up. I spoke to their head dude, a guy named Mack. He told me to come down the next day, since they were organizing a rally in front of an abortion clinic in a suburb outside Pittsburgh. That mean it would not be at the clinic where I'd had my abortion.

But the address he gave me to meet at was almost in downtown Pittsburgh. I had to take a bus to get there since dad was at work and my car was still out of commission. Besides, I'd lost my license to drive because of my suicide attempts.

After I went into the suicide center, Dad had hired a part time nurse to take care of mom while he was at work. I have no idea how he afforded it. It was handy now though, since I knew I'd go crazy if I had to sit in that house all day, with mom just staring vacantly into space. I felt guilty but grateful as I left mom with the nurse that day and took the bus from Cranberry down to the Burgh.

It was a long bus ride. It reminded me of that other bus ride I'd taken, the day after spending the night at Clarice's house. On that occasion, what mom had said about stopping Jonathon's heartbeat had filled my mind the whole journey, and I'd had to fight to keep it out. The familiarity of now being on the bus again threatened to do the same thing to me once more. I sighed deeply and frowned as I realized I had to once again forgive myself, since these memories had stirred up the old, familiar self-loathing I knew only too well.

When I got to the address Mack gave me it turned out to be a deserted video rental store, from the days before Redbox. There were lots of people milling around as I entered, young and old. There were also signs and posters all over with anti-abortion slogans on them. It gave me both a sense of discomfort and joy to know I was joining this group, to fight hated abortions. The discomfort of course was since I had had an abortion myself. But I had continued my Bible reading, so in a way I saw myself like the Apostle Paul who used to try and murder Christians before he became one.

Mack turned out to be an old fellow who looked like he could be my grandpa. As I came up to him he was discussing the upcoming rally with half a dozen men and women.

"Now remember," he said firmly, "there can be absolutely no physical contact with anyone going into the abortion clinic. That would violate the law Clinton signed back in '94. So don't touch anyone. We can't prevent them from going in. And we need to be careful not to say anything to them that could be interpreted as a threat. That would be a violation of the law too. I don't want any of you ending up in jail."

A chill went through my heart. Jail! Is that what might happen with this rally? Still, it was worth it if it would help stop abortions. There was nothing I wasn't willing to do.

"What about the new city ordinance, about how we can't get closer than 50 feet from the clinic?" asked a lady.

Mack grunted in disgust. "It's probably unconstitutional, as a violation of free speech under the First Amendment. But we'll abide by it." He shrugged. "Ever since the Supreme Court handed down Roe v. Wade in '73 and forced abortion to be legal in all 50 states, it has sometimes been reluctant to fully enforce free speech rights of protestors at abortion clinics. I guess that makes sense, since it's hard for the same court to both enforce abortion and free speech against abortion at the same time. Frankly, we'd be less likely to get thrown in jail if we were protesting poisoning whales than butchering human fetuses. But such is the state of the law in this country."

There was a murmur of disapproval from the group. "It's a bit different in Australia," said one man in a distinctly foreign accent. "You can demonstrate the same as any other organization."

"I wish that was true here," said Mack. "I suppose it is to some degree, since the lower federal courts are better at enforcing the free speech laws equitably for all demonstrating groups. Anyway, Australia legalized abortion by legislative action and voice of the people. The United States is the only country on earth that legalized abortion by a 7 to 2 vote of a court, even though the court ruling overturned abortion laws made by millions of people in almost all 50 states. We need everyone we can get to fight and turn the tables back around again."

There was another murmur from the crowd. I hadn't known any of this, of course. Is that really how it became legal in America? By a court decision of a few nutty judges? I thought it was some act of Congress.

"Americans like to think they're a pretty enlightened bunch," continued Mack, who was apparently quite good at speech making. "They think they're far superior to ancient Romans who sent people they didn't like to feed the lions, or the ancient Aztecs who sacrificed their children to their Gods. But the truth is, abortion is no different. Aborted children are sacrificed for the God of sexual gratification. Sex is more important than life. Sounds disgusting, but some people actually think that way. And there are 1.2 million abortions in America every year to prove it, with an estimated 42 million worldwide each year. They estimate that a billion babies have been aborted since 1980."

My stomach lurched as I heard this. How could this be possible! Were there really that many stupid people in the world? A billion aborted babies? Over a million a year in America? It was unthinkable!

Mack gave a few more instructions then disbursed the group. After that I went right up to him.

"Mack?" I said, shaking his hand. "I'm Kate. I called yesterday about joining your group."

He looked at me curiously for a second. "I see," he said. Something in his response didn't quite add up.

"What's wrong?" I asked. "Did I get here too late for the rally? Can't I go with the others?"

Mack looked at me for a minute without saying anything. Then he gently took my elbow and steered me over to the far corner of the room where our conversation would not be overheard. He suddenly startled me by asking, "How long since your abortion?"

"How did you know?" I blurted. "Does it look that obvious? Is it written in my face or something?"

"No, not at all," said Mack with a sad smile. "I've just been in this business a long time. I can usually spot them. They've been through hell and back with what they did, and want to make up for it somehow. So they shoot off to join an anti-abortion group. Am I right?"

I nodded. "Are there really that many girls like that?" I asked.

"Not all that many," he answered. "But enough for me to see the pattern." He let out a long breath. "And also enough for me to know that I can't use you right now. Maybe next year."

"Can't use me?" I blurted loudly, my heart sinking. "Why?"

"Look," he said patiently while straightening his glasses. "You're going through a recovery and healing process right now. You've reached a point where you want to do something--to get involved, and end the evil that shattered your life. It's good you feel that way, but my experience tells me if you join a group like mine right now it could cause you harm. Your own wounds are too fresh right now. You need more time to heal. Otherwise you can get scarred."

"Scarred?" I repeated dumbly. "I don't get it."

He smiled blandly. "The anti-abortion activist thing is a brutal environment. It can turn even a kindly housewife into a hardened woman, condemning others when she should be learning to love them instead. It's 100 times harder for someone like you, still recovering from the shock of abortion to avoid becoming harsh too. What you really need right now is an environment of love and service, not combat."

I frowned. "You don't know what I need!" I said firmly. "I want to do this. I HAVE to do this! I was listening when you told all those statistics on abortion a minute ago, and you didn't mention loving people then!"

"True," he said with a rueful smile. "But I say what I need to say, depending on my audience. That bunch needed some fire put in their bones, to help them make it through their six hour shift of total boringness while holding signs. You don't need that, since you've got plenty enough fire already. But what they need and I need and you need and we all need in this world, whether we're for abortion or against it, is more love and kindness. Love solves more problems than arguments, you know."

I frowned at him. "Well, whether that's true or not," I said slowly, "I'm here now and I want to be put to work. You can't turn me down!"

"Oh, yes I can," he answered casually. "I know you'll resent me for it, and probably just go out and find another anti-abortion organization to join. But right now I can't use you. Maybe next year after more time has passed since your abortion. In the meantime, I'd advise you to go out and improve your chances of healing by getting away from the subject of abortion for awhile and serving in other ways. There's lots of ways you can, you know."

My lip quivered. "You're really, actually turning me down?" I said in disbelief. "You just told all those people the cause needs as many people as it can get! And now you're turning me down?"

Mack took out a piece of paper and a pen and hastily wrote something down. "Here," he said, handing it to me. "Go see Peter. He can use you, I'm sure."

"Peter?" I asked questioningly. "Is he the leader of another anti-abortion group?"

"Not exactly," said Mack. "But he is the leader of a group that needs volunteers." He looked deeply into my eyes. "Trust me. I've seen this all before. Just go see Peter. He can use you, and I know it'll be a lot better for you."

I stared dumbly at the paper. Before I could say another word, Mack sauntered away. "Hey Joe, how about you and Sally making a half dozen more of those fetus posters." He called out. Our discussion was clearly at an end.

Stunned, I walked slowly out of the building and wandered down the street. This was positively weird. Here I was, ready, willing and able to do anything to end abortion, and some old guy who didn't even know me told me to forget it and do something else instead! How did he know what was best for me? THIS was the best therapy I could have--I was sure of it! What better way to get over my abortion than to fight against further abortions?

Well, I guess that meant I'd have to go searching online again to find another anti-abortion group to join. I just hoped its leader wasn't as weird as Mack.

I looked down at the paper in my hand. Peter. Mack thought some guy named Peter could use me for something. The address was close by, and I was already here in town. It was a long bus ride back, with nothing but mom staring vacantly into space when I got home. What would it hurt if I just went over there and saw what type of organization Peter was running? Then I could go home and look online for another anti-abortion group.

So, silly me, I went wandering down the street not knowing what I was getting into or what type of group Peter was running.

MAY 24

It didn't take long to find the address Mack had given me. But as I looked at the place I thought he must have written it down wrong. The place was an old, run-down house with broken windows and a sagging front door that looked like it might fall off its hinges any second. It was obvious the place was deserted and no one lived here. Mack must have been off his nut.

A young guy was sitting on the front step of the abandoned house. He wore a black leather jacket and black jeans, and his hair stood straight up in a spiky mohawk. He had multiple piercings--two through his lips, one in his nose, and three in his ears--and a shiny chain hung down from his belt. I also noticed a few tattoos on his hands and arms. In short he looked like a typical gang member you'd NEVER want to see coming toward you in a dark alley.

"You looking for someone?" he called out to me.

"No, not really," I said hastily, shoving the paper in my pocket. "I was just walking by."

"Looked to me like you were trying to find this house," he said casually as he got up off the step and started to saunter toward me. His chain made a jangling sound as he walked. Seeing a movement behind him, I suddenly realized there was another boy inside the house. No, make that two. Both started to come out onto the porch.

I suddenly started to feel frightened. Why had Mack sent me into gang territory? Did he want me to get mugged? "I was NOT trying to find this house," I said firmly. Then I turned to run.

"Hey, Peter," called out one of the boys as he came out of the house. To my surprise the boy looked nothing like Peter at all, but was plainly dressed and average looking. So was the other boy who came out behind him. They looked like they'd just stepped out of the halls of my old high school. "When are we going? Isn't it time yet?" one of them asked.

Peter didn't answer, but just stood there looking at me. For my part, I just stood there staring back at him. I must have looked kind of silly with my leg twisted around as if I was going to start running like crazy. But I just stood there frozen like a statue. Something about this whole picture didn't quite add up.

"Did someone send you?" asked Peter, his lip piercings wobbling in a bizarre sort of way while he talked. "Was it Shermy or Mrs. Goodhouse or Mack?"

"Mack," I blurted without thinking.

Peter broke into a grin that revealed a broken front tooth. "Good old Mack. Always watching out for me and sending me someone new."

"Peter!" came a girl's voice suddenly from the house. Startled, I looked around to see a girl about my age standing there. Like the two boys next to her, she looked pretty average, as if she had just come from my old high school. She definitely did not look like a gang member. But

~ 142 ~

right now she was looking at Peter with a big frown. "If we don't go now there won't be enough time to finish the job! Let's go, already!"

Peter just shrugged. "Just wanted to wait, to see who else might show up." Then he winked at me, making his eye piercing bob up and down. "And someone did, see?"

"I think I have to be going," I said noncommittally, suddenly not sure what to do.

"What's your name?" asked Peter, hooking his thumbs into the belt loops of his pants, so he could lift up his chains.

"Kate," I responded.

"Want to join us, Kate?" he asked. "We're about to go out and do a little job. Won't take long."

"What kind of job?" I asked, my curiosity getting the best of me.

"Just a little job," he said mysteriously. "Me and the 'J Raiders' here do all kinds of jobs all over. It'll be well worth your while."

The only 'little jobs' I could imagine him doing were all illegal. I turned to go again. But at that moment the girl on the porch yelled out, "Will you cut it out, Peter? Why are you always trying to scare people?" She came rapidly down the steps and out the gate, then took my arm. "Why don't you come along with us?" she asked. "It's not far away, and it shouldn't take long." She started to push me down the sidewalk while Peter and the two boys came along behind us. I stumbled along, still not sure this was a good idea.

"Where are we going?" I asked.

"To Mrs. Font's house," said the girl. "She's 92 and can't see well. We're going to work over her house."

I yanked my arm away. "No way!" I yelled. Peter suddenly burst out laughing. "Now who's scaring who, Janell?" he asked the girl through his glee.

She blushed and smiled in embarrassment. "It's not what you think," she said hastily. "We're going to help her. She needs her lawn mowed one last time before the winter snow hits, and inside there'll probably be dishes to wash and some cleaning. She's just too old to do it herself."

I looked quizzically from Janell to Peter, then back to Janell again. "But, didn't he say you guys are the J Raiders or something? Isn't that a gang?"

Janell rolled her eyes. "That's just a name he made up," she said. She glanced back at him with a frown. "Probably just to scare people. But it's not what you think."

Peter smiled in a gawky way and spread his arms wide in a needless dramatic gesture, as if he was hugging the whole world. "We're the 'Jesus Raiders,' sweet Kate!" he said happily. "We swoop in and do stuff and make people sorry they ever laid eyes on us!"

"They are not sorry!" said Janell, reaching out and hitting him on his arm. "They're grateful. All of them. Why do you always have to be so dramatic and stupid?"

Peter just rolled his eyes straight up, and I found myself wondering if he was crazy, or if he'd addled his mind with drugs at some point in the past. "Just acting like I did when I was in a REAL gang!" he said dramatically, looking up at the sky.

"Oh, poo!" replied Janell, hitting him again. "You were never in a real gang. You're no more of a gang member than me!"

Peter looked hurt. "Of course I was in a gang! I was in the Wolverines. We nearly killed three people!"

"Probably from making them laugh to death," Janell said with a frown. She turned and propelled me faster down the sidewalk. "What a nut!" she said under her breath.

"So, who is he?" I asked in a half whisper, my curiosity now thoroughly aroused. To my annoyance Peter came bounding up behind us and hovered a listening ear over our shoulders. "Yes, Janell, who am I?" he asked curiously.

"You're a nut!" cried Janell, turning and punching him again. But she smiled as she did it this time, and I noticed she didn't hit too hard. Then he just bounded away, doing a quirky little jig as he went as if he had completely lost his senses.

That was my introduction to Peter, and his 'gang' of 'J Raiders.' As I soon found out, his gang had almost 100 members in it, and all of them were young people like me. They came from all over, and were referred by pastors, school counselors, parents or friends of Peter's. A few were rough or troubled kids who probably needed therapy, but most of them just wanted to help. All of them were used for one purpose--to provide the manpower to serve people in need all over the Pittsburgh area.

And Peter ALWAYS had a project for his 'gang' to do. That day we completely cleaned up old Mrs. Font's place. The next day we helped tear old shingles off a church roof, so new ones could be installed. The day after that we rolled old fashioned wheel-barrows--yes wheel barrows!--full of donated canned goods to the homeless shelter. Peter's projects never ended, and every one of them helped put someone, or some group, back on their feet.

I soon saw that Peter was every bit the nut Janell said he was. He had a quirky but effective way of keeping the kids who needed therapy in line. But for the rest of us he was just totally quirky, never doing anything like a normal person and often saying and doing some of the most ridiculous things. I saw this the following week when we went to an orphanage and he tied a mop to his head and danced the funky chicken for all the laughing, screaming kids. And I saw it again on our way to paint Mr. McGruder's house, when Peter jumped on top of a police car for no reason and started to sing the Star Spangled Banner. My heart nearly stopped and I thought we'd end up in jail for sure, but the policeman just got out of his car laughing and told Peter to get off his roof.

And I saw it again when we went to the hospital the next Sunday, to a special ward of very sick people. He seemed unusually quiet as he and his 'gang' caught the bus from that dumpy old house where he apparently lived and went out to the hospital. There were seven of us this time, and Janell and the other two boys I'd first seen were not among them. When we got to the hospital Peter was still quiet. He hadn't told us where we were going or what we were going to do there. He'd only asked (the day before, when he asked who could come with him) to bring a handkerchief and a kazoo.

"A kazoo?" I'd asked in surprise, leaving a streak on a window I was washing for Mrs. Shelley at the time.

"Bless you," he responded nonsensically. "But to answer your question, a kazoo is a small musical instrument you can buy at most dollar stores. Bring one," he'd said, smiling at me mysteriously. And yes, when I later went to the dollar store, they did indeed sell kazoos, which make a rather annoying buzzing sound when you blow in them.

So here we were at the hospital. I nearly fainted when Peter led us upstairs and then through a door labeled 'Terminal Illness Ward.' So did the other six kids. We all felt distinctly uncomfortable as we passed through the doors, and were especially unnerved at how quiet it was. You could practically hear your own heartbeat.

The quiet was suddenly shattered by Peter. "Hallooo everyone!" he cried in a horrifyingly loud voice, causing us all to jump. "I know you're all just dying to see us--and we're here!" Nurses came flying out of hallways and doors faster than ants out of an anthill that's just been stepped on. They all 'shushed' Peter of course, but the loony paid no attention.

"The show will start in 5 minutes folks!" he bellowed at the top of his considerable lungs.

"So be ready. We know you can't come to us, so we'll come to you."

By now the nurses were grabbing Peter's arms and shirt and chains with the intent of forcibly throwing him out. The seven of us just stood there not knowing what to do. But a laughing doctor suddenly appeared, to Peter's great relief.

"Peter!" he called out in a loud voice that made several nurses wince, since they apparently preferred it to be quiet. "Glad you could make it. Is this your kazoo band?" The doctor looked at us all knowingly, while we just stared stupidly back at him. Peter just nodded his head up and down, grinning like a sick mongoose.

What followed next was total, chaotic insanity. Peter 'tuned us up' on our kazoos and made us play, and the noise was worse than a catfight. Then he marched us through the room of each patient, where we were horrified to find people literally on their deathbeds. Most of them were old, but sadly a few were young. They were all hooked up to IVs and some of them to oxygen, and most of them just lay there limply looking at us. But every one of them smiled as we filed past making our horrible racket.

After that, we spend the next two hours going into individual rooms and talking to them. Now I understood why Peter had said to not only bring a kazoo but also a handkerchief. It was like having my guts wrenched out to see these people literally dying before my eyes. We talked with them of course, trying vainly to cheer them up. But I could see that the thing that had cheered them most was the insane kazoos. Several of them told us they wanted to hear our kazoo band again.

One lady in particular was very emphatic. "Young man," she said to Peter who was standing next to me by her bedside as we looked down on her pasty, white face. "You look like a hoodlum. A disgusting hoodlum with all those piercings. But I'm grateful to you. Do you know, it's probably been five months since I laughed. Five months!"

"Then we'll come back in another five months and do it again," said Peter insanely.

"I won't be here," she said sadly. "Won't you do it again now? They say I've only got 'till the end of the week."

"The end of the week, is that all?" bellowed Peter with horrible irreverence, making her smile. "Why listen to kazoos then? By the end of the week you'll be listening to a heavenly choir, and it'll be much better!"

"No, it won't," responded the lady, shaking her head weakly. "No sound could be more angelic. Do it again, won't you? For me? One last time."

So we did. In fact, Peter and I played a kazoo duet that sounded truly awful. And suddenly the lady started to laugh and laugh as if it was the funniest thing in the world. And with Peter dancing around like he was the pied piper, I could see why. As for me though, he looked a bit blurry since my eyes had unaccountably gotten rather watery.

I never thought I would be sad to leave a 'terminal illness ward,' but I was that night. As we walked down the hall everyone was smiling, and nurses were trailing after us thanking us again and again. Peter seemed absolutely ecstatic, and was not at all sad as he'd been coming in.

"I always feel so much better when I come here," he said. "Sad on the way in, but happy on the way out. They lift me up, you know that? Those people make me feel better."

I just stared at Peter in amazement. It seemed impossible to me that he was clueless about who had made who feel better.

But the people in the hospital that night knew.

MAY 25

So there, journal! Did you see that? There was hardly anything in my last entry about abortion! Hardly anything at all! My therapist would be extremely pleased. And Mack had been right after all. What I needed was the 'Jesus raiders,' and the chance to do something worthwhile that didn't remind me of abortion every day. I never forgot my abortion of course, and I still had the dreams of Jonathon (but no knives in the dreams anymore, thank heavens!) and I still had to keep forgiving myself about 50 times a day. But working with Peter was restoring my soul. I felt in a way that my life had started over, and that it was truly a wonderful life, and was a life worth living after all.

There were difficult moments of course. Mom was still as bad as ever, and Oscar was still missing. I had to report for evaluation once a week since I'd spent all that time on suicide watch. And Clarice had Michael born to her in Florida and sent me a picture--and true to my word I threw her letter away unopened. I knew I wasn't ready for that just yet. But I also knew I was progressing, that things were getting better, and that someday I might be able to handle receiving a letter from her. The main reason was because of love and forgiveness, Jesus and Peter.

I found out one day just how far I'd come while I was on my way to Peter's dumpy house for another one of his 'gang jobs.' I was still not allowed to drive because of my suicide history, and my car was still totaled in that accident I'd had anyway. So I took the bus down to Peter's house like normal. As I walked along the street towards his place I saw what looked at first like a lumpy bag of old clothes someone had tossed in the gutter. But as I got closer I saw this was not a bundle of clothes--it was a human being. And as I arrived at the side of this person, I sucked in my breath in surprise.

It was none other than Dorothy Malk, that awful lady I'd seen that day at the abortion clinic. She lay there as if she was dead. Just like before she reeked of alcohol, and her clothes were unkempt and dirty. Her hair was straggled over her closed eyes, and there was a rash down the side of her face that had not been there when I'd seen her last.

In a rush, the horror of that day when I first saw her at the abortion clinic came crashing back into my mind. I felt an involuntary urge to suddenly throw up as her vivid descriptions of abortions took over my memory.

My initial impulse was to turn and run, to put as much distance as I could between myself and that awful woman. It made my blood curdle to think of the babies she had killed in the late terms of her pregnancies, and how callous she was about having done so.

But as I looked down at her, whether because of Peter and the 'Jesus Raiders,' or my reading of the Bible, or what I'd learned about forgiveness--I don't know what caused it, but suddenly I felt a wave of compassion and pity for her. She suddenly didn't look a demon in the flesh as I'd thought before, but more like a worn out old woman who had made many bad choices, but who still needed love.

I kneeled down and tapped her shoulder. "Dorothy," I called softly. "Are you all right?"

She stirred and groaned, then stretched stiffly. After that she opened one eye and looked up at me.

"Who are you?" she asked in that gravel voice of hers.

"A friend," I answered simply. "Are you all right? Do you need help getting to your house?"

"Ain't got no house, sister," said Dorothy, struggling unsuccessfully to sit up. "No house except this here gutter!" She looked up at me again with one eye, and I realized suddenly she couldn't open the other one because of the rash on that side of her face.

I bit my lip, not sure what to do. "Is there something I can do to help you?" I asked.

"Now that you mention it, you could give me a little something to freshen up my spirits." She looked at me expectantly and held out her hand. At first I was clueless what she meant, but then I understood.

"No, I think you've had enough to drink," I replied.

"'Taint for drink, honey," she responded. "Just for a bite to eat." I looked around the street we were on. There were two bars nearby, and also a seedy looking hot dog stand not far away. "I'll buy you a hot dog then," I said firmly. It seemed pretty obvious that any money I gave her would not go to food with those bars so close.

She frowned, but just shrugged. Then she struggled unsuccessfully to rise to her feet. This time I reached out and tried to help her, taking hold of her soiled, stinking, alcohol soaked clothes. Between the two of us she staggeringly made it. And boy was she heavy!

"Thanks, toots," she said brusquely. "But you don't need to buy me no food. I can get my own. Just give me some money."

"No, I'll buy it for you," I said, shaking my head. "Here, I'll help you get over there." Together we staggered toward a bench next to the hot dog stand, looking for all the world like two drunks who'd had a night out on the town (and one of us had!)

We finally made it. After I got her on the bench and made sure she wouldn't fall off, I went over and bought us both a hot dog. Even though I wasn't that hungry, I decided it might not be polite for her to eat alone.

"Thanks, sweets," she said as she took the hot dog from me. She ate it ravenously, as if she had never eaten before. I suddenly felt guilty for having taken a bite out of my hot dog, which I could have given to her. But that problem was easily solved by going to buy her another one.

After she finished she gave me a quizzical look. "Do I know you?" she asked curiously. "Seems like I've seen you someplace before."

"We may have met once," I answered vaguely. Then I changed the subject. "Where will you go now?"

"Don't know, sweets," she said huskily. "Got no place to call my own. And this bum leg won't let me walk far. That's why that spot of gutter became my home."

I shook my head. This would never do. But I was clueless about what I could do to help.

Peter. The thought suddenly leapt into my head, and I knew instantly what to do. I turned to Dorothy. "Will you stay here and wait for me for a few minutes?" I asked anxiously. "I've got to go talk to a friend who can help you."

Dorothy smiled ruefully. "I'm not going anywhere toots." Then she glanced at the glowering hot dog salesman who was not pleased that she was on the bench usually used by his customers. "'Cept maybe back to my gutter."

"No, stay right here," I said firmly. I frowned over at the hot dog salesman, who looked away in embarrassment. "This is a public bench and you've got a right to sit here. I'll be back soon." Before she could answer I took off.

I raced down the street as fast as I could go. I had been a bit late already, and Peter may have already left for his 'job.' If he wasn't there I simply had no idea what I would do. But as I rounded the corner, I felt a wave of relief as I saw that he was still lounging on his front step. A few kids were waiting around, rather impatiently, wanting to get moving.

"Peter!" I said breathlessly as I came up to the step. "There's a woman back there that needs your help!"

"Really?" said Peter, smiling in that gawky way of his that made his lip piercings wobble.

Then he winked at me. "Are you sure it's not YOUR help she needs?"

I frowned at him. He could be annoying and impossible at times. "No, she needs YOUR help, because she can't walk and has no home, and she's still half drunk and more than half starved--and she just needs help!"

He winked at me again. "All right, Katey-Matey, then let's you and me go help her!" I rolled my eyes. I hated it when he called me 'Katey-Matey,' which he'd started to do quite often lately.

"Be back shortly guys," called out Peter to the waiting 'gang' members. "Then we'll go over and help put up that wall I was telling you about." None of them seemed to mind his leaving with me, since putting up a wall sounded a bit daunting.

When we got back to Dorothy, she had moved back to 'her' gutter. I glared at the hot dog salesman (after all, I'd bought three of his hot dogs!), but he just looked away.

"Howdy, Ma'am," said Peter with a smile as he came up to her. Dorothy just stared up at him in surprise.

"You talking to me?" she said roughly.

"I don't see any other ma'am in any other gutter around here," said Peter, looking around in all the gutters. Dorothy screwed up her face in further surprise, then started to laugh. It sounded like a broken washing machine.

"Ain't you cute," she chirped. "Wanna get married?"

"Don't have the time," said Peter casually. "Kate here tells me you've got no home and can't hardly walk. Is that true?"

"Yep," said Dorothy, almost as if she was proud of it. "What's it to you?" Peter just shrugged. Then he pulled out a cell phone I had never seen before. I was surprised that it looked pretty fancy. He dialed a number and waited a second.

"Hello?" he said into the phone. "Delancy? I've got one for you. Yep, can't move. Needs medical attention, besides a place to stay." He suddenly looked around for a street sign. "We're on first street, near Highland. Right. See ya."

Dorothy was struggling to rise with a scowl on her face. "I don't know who you called, but I'm not waitin' around to find out," she said in a huff.

"Just the County Aide," said Peter.

"Humph!" sniffed Dorothy. "I been to them before. Don't like 'em."

"Good for you!" said Peter for no reason as he reached out and shook her hand. "We'll just wait a minute until they get here. They can help with that leg problem of yours, and it won't cost you a dime."

"Eh?" said Dorothy, looking at him curiously. She wheezed and coughed, then said, "Well ... I suppose I could let them take a look at it ..."

Seeing Peter in action had given me a sudden, brilliant idea. He seemed to always know just what to do and what to say when no one else did. And I knew of one person who I and others had been trying to reach for a very long time that maybe--just maybe--he could help.

Peter showed up at my house right on schedule. "Fancy place you got here," he said, looking all around in admiration as he came into our front hall. "Doesn't hold a candle to my house of course, but maybe with time you'll get this place there."

I smiled at his nonsense, since his house in Pittsburgh looked like it was about to collapse. My heart was giddy with hope that he could do something for Mom, so any idiotic thing he said would make me smile. Dad had hired a stream of specialists to examine Mom, but none had been able to help. Some had suggested that he put her in an institution. However he had steadfastly refused to do so, insisting he would look after her himself. It hadn't been easy on him, but with the help of the part-time nurse he'd hired he'd been able to get by. It had also helped when I came home from suicide watch to help out too.

"She's upstairs," I said, starting to head up. I had been staying with mom today, since I had arranged for the nurse to be gone when Peter came. I didn't know how she would react to him, since his strange and rather frightening appearance sometimes tended to worry people.

"Hold on there, Katey-Matey," he said irritatingly. "You haven't told me what this is all about." He looked at me expectantly.

"I did too!" I replied firmly. "I told you she just stares into space and doesn't say much. And she thinks I'm dead, even when I'm right there in the room with her." I put my hands on my hips, frowning.

He just shook his head. "That's not good enough. I know there's more to her story than that. I won't see her 'till I know what it is." He casually strolled over and sat on the couch. I was suddenly glad Dad was at work, since he'd probably freak out if he saw Peter in his black outfit with all his body piercings and tattoos lounging on his couch.

"There's no more story than that," I lied. "It just happened to her one day."

"What day?" he asked.

I looked down at the ground. "Just a day," I answered. "I just came home and it happened." There was an awkward silence for a moment. When I looked up he was smiling at me expectantly.

"And ..." he said simply.

What choice did I have? I'd never had any desire to tell him my story, and I felt uncomfortable and embarrassed to do so now. But it obviously had to be done, or he'd never go up to see her. And in a strange way, I knew somehow that he would not judge me or condemn me when he found out that I was the cause of my Mom's condition, and that I'd killed Jonathon. After all, this was Peter who accepted everyone just the way they were.

He just sat there patiently and listened. And I was right--he didn't seem surprised or shocked or disappointed when I explained about my abortion, and my haunting dreams of Jonathon, and then how Mom fell into her condition when she found out what I'd done.

Then I explained about Mom's abortion where she thought she'd killed me, and how she was convinced I was dead. He just sat there and sucked on a butterscotch candy, making squeaky, annoying sounds with this teeth as he did so.

When I was finally done I looked at him expectantly. "Well?" I said rather harshly, my face red from the agony of reliving that horrid story once more. "Are you finally ready to go up, now that you know all the family secrets, and all about my horrible past?"

"Have you had a horrible past?" he asked in genuine surprise. I gritted my teeth. "Yes! I just told you! I killed my baby for no reason! And that caused Mom to fall into this condition of hers, and she's slowly dying too! And it's all my fault!"

He got smilingly to his feet and tapped me gently on the arm as he headed for the stairs. "You'll have to tell me about your horrible past sometime, Katey-Matey. I still can't figure where you get that idea from." Before I could answer his nonsense he bounded up the stairs two at a time and went into Mom's room, while I rushed to keep up with him.

"Howdy, Katey-Matey's Mom!" he said cheerfully as he charged into the room. "I understand you had an abortion and killed your baby! Is that right?"

I stood in the door so shocked I nearly fainted. What was he doing? How could he SAY such a disgusting thing?! Didn't he know approaching her like that would shock her horribly?

Apparently he did. She opened her eyes wide, staring at him. For a second there was an awkward silence in the room. Then she suddenly screeched, "Yes! You're right! That's exactly what I did! I killed my baby! My baby Kate! Finally someone believes me!"

Peter went over and picked up both of her waxy, dead-fish hands. "Would you like to see her, even though she's dead?" he asked intently. Mom's eyes suddenly filled with tears and she nodded her head vigorously that she did.

"Now, don't be too surprised she doesn't look like a baby anymore," said Peter. "After all, it's been a long time since you killed her. 18 years, in fact."

"Has it really?" said Mom in surprise.

"Yes," he said simply. Then he nodded toward where I was standing in the doorway. "That's her over there. That's your baby Kate, only all grown up. What do you think of her?"

Mom's eyes just stared at me in a watery way. I bit my lip in frustration. This wasn't working! Every day for months now I'd come in and told her I was her daughter. What had possessed me to think that Peter could solve this problem, even with his weird genius?

"Kate?" Mom said in a shrill voice. She looked back at Peter. "That's Kate?" He shook his head that it was.

"But I killed Kate," she said, just like she always did. "I killed her, so that can't be her. Besides, I see that girl every day."

"Yes, you did kill her," said Peter casually, as if it really didn't matter. "You did indeedy. But she wanted to see you so much, she came back. In fact, she came back a long time ago. And then you raised her from a little girl. All those dreams you had about how wonderful it would be if your baby could come back came true! And you raised her, and there she is. That's why you see her every day. That girl is Kate. She loves you so much she came back from the dead. She came back from the dead because of the power of Jesus. She forgives you and so does Jesus. Kate's not upset you killed her. Not at all. She loves you. And she came back from the dead just to be with you."

Mom just looked at me, her lips quivering. "It can't be ..." she said slowly. "But I killed her. I did." She put her hands to her head. "I remember going to the abortion clinic ..."

"And remember how you came back and how upset you were at what you'd done," continued Peter. "And then suddenly she came back to life, even though she was dead! She really did! It was a miracle from Jesus. She was truly killed, but then she came back to life! And then you got to raise her. You knew you didn't deserve it, but you got to raise her anyway. And there she is, right over there. There she is. That's your Kate."

Everything in the room was suddenly very blurry. For no good reason, I felt as if my heart was breaking. Everything Peter had said to her was true, of course, in a way. But somehow his saying it brought the reality crashing back for me that it was not the same with me and Jonathon. I'd killed him dead. He never came back. He never did, and he never would. There was no such miracle for Jonathon and me. And it was because of me that he was dead, and--"

"Hey, there, Katey-Matey," came a distant voice through the fog of my tears. I felt someone take my hand. "I can guess what you're thinking--and you're wrong! He comes back every night, Katey-Matey. Every night in your dreams. And he forgives you, and loves you just as you are. And some day because of Jesus he will live again--he'll come back from the dead too! Jesus can bring anyone back from the dead, and he'll bring Jonathon back too. I promise you, he will."

I broke down at that point, starting to blubber like a stupid little girl. I vaguely felt Peter lead me over to my Mom and put my hands on hers. "Have a nice cry-fest!" came his nonsensical voice, fading toward the door. "And don't forget we're cleaning out Mr. Phelps's dog pen tomorrow, Katey-Matey!" And then the crazy, wonderful fool was gone.

For the next hour Mom and I just hugged each other and balled our eyes out. And in my ear, over and over, Mom kept saying, "Kate! Kate! My darling Kate! Oh, Kate, I love you so. Oh, Kate, I'm so sorry for what I did, but I'm so happy you came back to me from the dead! Oh, Kate! You're alive again!"

MAY 31

Well, journal, now you know. Now you know how Mom finally got past the mental block I'd put in her mind when she found out about my abortion. Peter did it. It was Peter's miracle. Mom started to improve from that hour, and although she still gets confused sometimes and finds herself wondering if I am alive or dead, she usually comes back out of it pretty quick after she sees me walk into the room.

Dad was ecstatic of course. He practically begged for me to take him to Peter so he could thank him. At first I resisted, since I was afraid the sight of Peter might shock Dad pretty bad. But Dad kept insisting so I finally allowed him to drive me down to Peter's house and they got to meet. And Dad didn't act shocked at all--just grateful. And then Peter recruited him to go help some orphan children the following Saturday.

As for me and Jonathon, Peter was right. He still visits me almost every night. Now I look forward to going to bed and dreaming, since I know I will probably get to see him. And in almost all my dreams he is smiling.

Yes, journal, it looks like the story has been told. My idiot therapist should be happy. Of course, Oscar still hasn't come back, but I keep hoping. And my car is still in the shop, but someday I will get it fixed and drive again, when I get my license back. And Mom is still not back to her normal housekeeping, but it will hopefully come someday. And I still have to forgive myself a few dozen times every day, especially when I go to the mall or the park and see young moms with their babies. But beside all those things, I'd say the story has been told.

But there is one more story to tell. A story that's sad in a way, but helps make sense out of a number of things.

It happened the day Peter called. He called me in the morning and asked if I would come down that afternoon, because he was getting a group together on a very special and very large service project. In fact he said it was probably the biggest so far. Naturally I agreed.

As I got off the bus that day I searched my brain, trying to figure out what it could be. After all, a project that big wouldn't likely just jump out of thin air. I'd been working with Peter long enough that I usually knew the various jobs which were coming up. In fact, I was one of his 'regulars' now, and he sometimes had me take charge of a group when he had a conflict of two service projects at once and couldn't go to both.

When I arrived at his shabby, broken down house, he was once more sitting on the front step waiting. I smiled when I saw him. He was such a crazy looking guy, and had an even crazier personality. But his heart was as big as the universe.

Janell showed up a minute later, and after that Fred and Harry, two of Peter's other regulars. He smiled at us all. And then he did something he'd never done before. "Come on into the kitchen," he said, as he turned and led the way through the broken-down door nearly falling off its hinges.

I glanced meaningfully at Janell, then followed with growing excitement. All of us in his gang had often speculated to each other about what the bowels of his house must look like inside. But all anyone had ever seen was the shabby, rotting front room just inside that broken-down door. Now the mystery of the rest of the house was finally about to be unveiled. As I followed him inside I was filled with a morbid curiosity to see how bad it was. I could tell Janell was too--and also that she was getting ready to ball him and tell him he needed to go live in a decent place.

The front room was a shambles of course, just as we'd seen it before. But then Peter pulled out a key and unlocked a door leading into the back part of the house. And when we walked through it, we felt like we'd stepped into another world.

It was fantastic! It was like a new house back here, with thick, gorgeous carpet and a new kitchen and new appliances. There was a family room right off the kitchen with a big screen TV and a fridge stocked with delicious foods. Never had I imagined Peter lived like this!

He looked at us all apologetically. "Sorry about this guys. I wouldn't have the house look like this, but my Uncle insisted. You see, he's kind of rich and he didn't like it when he saw this place when I first moved in. So he insisted on fixing it up for me. But I never use it much-- and I almost never watch the big screen TV! Honest!"

Janell and I smiled at his embarrassment. Cocky Peter, always so sure of himself was now

truly blushing with shame--at being well off!
The guy was an obvious fruitcake!

"Now," he said as he took a seat at a
beautifully carved kitchen table and motioned
for us to sit down too. "I suppose you're all
wondering why I called you here--isn't that a
great line? Somebody ought to use it in a movie
or a book, or something."

Janell giggled, and I found it necessary to
concentrate very hard on a spot on my shoe so I
wouldn't join her. Suddenly Peter pulled four
file folders off an empty chair next to him and
handed one to each of us.

"Now Janell will take east Pittsburgh
during the six months I'm gone, and Fred will
take the south and Harry the west, and--

"Gone!" shrieked all four of us together.
Then we were all talking at once.

"Where are you going?"

"WHY are you going?"

"You can't just leave us here!"

"There's no way we can do this without
you!"

"Everyone's going to freak out when they
learn you're gone!"

Peter held up his hands for silence.
"Golly, guys," he said casually, "if I didn't know
better, I'd think you were troubled about
something. Don't know why. I chose you four
because I knew you could handle things while I
was gone, and also because--"

"But you can't go!" shrieked both Janell
and I together. "We won't let you!" I added
firmly.

"Well, that's nice, it really is," said Peter. "But I don't think the state police will be convinced when they come tomorrow to take me away."

We all froze as if we'd been doused with a ton of ice. Then we started talking again.

"State police!" said Fred.

"What did you do?" blurted Harry.

"This is impossible!" said Janell. I didn't say anything. Peter just held up his hand for silence again. Then an unaccountable look of sadness crossed his face.

"I decided on you four to handle things while I'm gone for two reasons. First, you're all very capable and will do a good job." Seeing us about to protest again that we knew we were NOT very capable and would undoubtedly flop without him, he raised both hands in the air for silence.

"The second reason I chose you four is a bit more sensitive," he continued. He looked at us for a moment. "I've tried very hard to avoid getting into personal matters before with any member of the gang, and I don't intend to start now. But sometimes personal things have to be discussed. I don't want to shock any of you, or for you to be shocked at each other. But as I've thought it through, I can't think of any other way to explain this than just the blunt approach. I chose you four specifically because each one of you knows what it feels like to think you were responsible for killing someone."

There was deathly silence in the kitchen. Incredible silence. It was only penetrated by the gentle humming of his refrigerator, and the gentle ticking of a large grandfather clock against the far wall.

"Now, I think I have your undivided attention, with no likelihood of interruption," said Peter with a smile. "Once again, I don't want any of you to feel uncomfortable, or to be wondering about WHY each of you knows what it feels like to believe you were responsible for killing someone. It's enough to know that's the case. Because you're all familiar with that feeling, and how horrible it is and how guilty it made you feel, I know you won't question or judge each other. And perhaps you won't question or judge me when you find out why I have to leave for six months--why the police are coming to take me. And if you don't question or judge me, then maybe you'll be willing to carry on my work while I'm gone."

We just stared at him. The awful reality of what he was telling us was starting to sink in, making us all feel very depressed. Why was this happening? Not Peter! Not him, of all people!

He suddenly smiled broadly. "Hey guys, cheer up! You look like a bunch of mice that just found out you ate moldy cheese! You've been through this! You learned the power of Jesus and the power of forgiveness, and especially the power of forgiving yourselves! You've seen the power of loving people, and how that heals you! I don't want you to become disillusioned about me and what I've done in the past, but hey--it's who I am. It's part of my past, just like it's part of yours."

He fiddled with the corner of Harry's file for a moment. We knew that he was now going to tell us what had happened in his past--who he'd killed. And I found myself wishing very much that he wouldn't.

"Janell, you were wrong," he said after a long pause. "I was a member of a gang once. It wasn't called the Wolverines, but it was an honest to goodness gang. In New York City. And one day there was a fight and a few people died. And when it all went through the courts, I was convicted of manslaughter."

To my surprise, tears were welling up in Peter's eyes. But I could tell he was determined to tell us his story. And I suddenly realized that at a different time and in a different way, each one of us had told him our story, about who we'd killed. For me, it had been that day I told him about my abortion when he came to help Mom.

"You see," he continued slowly, "my brother was in this gang, and he got me to join. I didn't want to. I didn't like violence. I hated it. So I never got into the fights. I avoided them. And I was planning to leave the city and the gang forever when this fight happened. All I needed was a few more months until I graduated from high school. But I never ended up graduating."

That sounded familiar.

"In this big fight I found myself fighting a guy I didn't want to fight. And it became increasingly clear to me that it was kill or be killed. And you know what?" His upper lip was trembling. "I struggled with that ..." He was having a hard time keeping his voice under control. "I wasn't sure I wanted his death on my conscience. I was scared, but I was starting to think maybe I should let him win the fight."

Janell gave him a weak smile. "I wasn't wrong, Peter. You were never a member of any gang."

He smiled back at her, probably wanting to make a joke of it like he usually did. But he couldn't. All he could do was continue his story.

"I pulled back my knife, since I was thinking I'd throw it on the ground," he said in a strained voice. "But somehow that action somehow distracted my opponent and then he slipped and fell on my knife ..."

He didn't need to say any more. We knew what had happened. And that bizarre question leapt into all of our minds that we'd asked ourselves in respect to our own killing. Was he responsible? Or was he innocent? Obviously he was innocent as far as we were concerned. But no one could deny he HAD been in a gang fight, and HAD been holding a knife that killed someone, and HAD been convicted in the courts ...

"Like I said, the conviction was for manslaughter," he said calmly. "I spent two and a half years in prison for it, then was released on parole with the condition of doing community service--which is what I've been doing here. But it was always understood that I would need to return for six more months of prison time, to fully complete my sentence. And tomorrow at 2:00 o'clock, that is what will happen."

We were all silent, each lost in our own thoughts. "Oh, Peter! Peter!" I found myself thinking. "I am SO sorry for you! I know just how you feel. I know precisely how you feel. And I am so sorry this happened to you."

There was no doubt everyone else around the table was thinking the same thing.

"It may or may not be best for the other members of the 'Jesus Raiders' to know why I'm gone--I'll leave it up to the four of you to decide, as to whether to tell them."

As I glanced quickly around the table, I had a strong suspicion the others felt as I did. They would NOT tell the true reason, since that would just prejudice other members of the club against him--members who, unlike us, would not understand because they had not been through it themselves. And it was only too obvious that is precisely why he had chosen us four to take over for him while he was gone.

He suddenly let out a long breath, as if he had been unable to breathe for some time. "Well, now that's done, I think you all understand what's expected of you. These folders contain many projects that have been lined up in each of your areas. You are responsible to arrange other projects in your areas as well, to keep the Jesus Raiders busy and active. I have no doubt everything will be running just dandy upon my return. In fact," he added with a wicked smile, "I'm partly tempted to not even return at all--"

"NO WAY!" we all shouted at once. "Don't even THINK about it!" said Janell, slugging his arm. He couldn't slug her back of course since she was a girl.

"No Janell," he said with a smile. "I would never even think about it. I've found my life's calling. I'm a 'lifer' with the J Raiders! You know darn well I'll be back."

Suddenly he turned and waved to the interior of his house. "This will be your headquarters. Use it freely."

After that, there wasn't much else to say. So he rather awkwardly showed us the rest of the elegantly remodeled house, and kindly let us raid his refrigerator. And then he 'just happened' to remember that Mrs. Jones was expected help in about an hour to paint her back porch ...

So there you have it, journal. The last story has been told, and my therapist will be ecstatic. Peter is gone now, and I'm doing my best to fill in for him in the North Pittsburgh area. It isn't easy. I never knew how hard he worked, or all he did. The poor guy must not have had time to sleep, handling all four areas of Pittsburgh by himself! No wonder he was never able to watch that big screen TV!

Jonathon is helping me do my job of course. He encourages me almost every night in my dreams. And I'd like to think that many times during the day he comes down as well, just to give me a little push, or a little bit of extra strength, or to put an encouraging thought into my mind.

Jonathon, oh Jonathon! If only I had let you live! It's true I never would have gotten to know Peter and the 'Jesus Raiders', but I would have happily traded that in an instant just to have you, and to hold you, and to love you. How I wish I had done things differently. Oh, how I wish I'd done things differently.

But I didn't. And I have finally come to terms with it, and have forgiven myself for it.

Thanks for your love Jonathon. And thanks for forgiving me, and helping me to forgive myself.

Next year, after Peter comes back, I'm going to go back to Mack. I think I'm almost ready to be an anti-abortion activist. I'm ready to stand firm for that position, but to do it in a spirit of love and compassion. Unfortunately there are a lot of Dorothy Macks still in the world. But rather than bash them over the head or yell at them, I'd rather love them instead--just love them while carrying forward my message, learned from painful experience, that abortion is very, very wrong.

And Jonathon will help me. I know he will.

To contact the author feel free to send an email to: duanelostler@gmail.com

OTHER BOOKS BY THE AUTHOR

<u>Nonfiction</u>

<u>The Ninth Amendment: Key to Understanding the Bill of Rights</u>. This book explains how the Ninth Amendment is the key to understanding rights in the United States. The founders created the Ninth Amendment to protect unlisted natural law rights as they were understood in their day. This amendment was never intended to allow future generations to create new rights. Rather, it was to safeguard the morality and natural rights of the founding generation.

<u>Judicial Activism: A Way to Overcome It</u>. Judicial activism in the U.S. occurs when a few Supreme Court judges decide public policy issues, which normally deal with rights. However, it would be better for the people to decide such issues through their elected representatives. This book proposes a way to remove judicial activism, by returning to an original view of the founding fathers that preferred legislative oversight of rights issues.

<u>Rights in America, Bills of Attainder and the Ninth Amendment</u>. While rights in America have always been cherished, many people today

misunderstand the source of their rights. They have come to believe that government is the grantor of rights. The flipside of this belief is that government can also take them away. Such a view conflicts with that of the founders, who gave us the ban on bills of attainder and 9th Amendment to forever protect our natural rights.

Our Sex Saturated Society. American society is obsessed with sex. This obsession has led to extreme results that would be considered appalling by prior generations, such as: rampant premarital sex which increases AIDS while decreasing trust and commitment between partners; gays/lesbians elevating sex to such an extreme it has become their god; and abortions in which innocent unborns are yanked out piece by piece.

False Worlds. A false world is like an apple full of worms. It appears juicy and attractive on the outside, but is in fact disgusting on the inside. This book discusses a number of false worlds masquerading as truth but which are in fact false to their core. Included are the false worlds of politics, international relations, law, sexual confusion (premarital sex, abortion and gayness), entertainment and pride.

The Anti Stupidity Book. Stupidity. What is it? Is it just something we see our neighbors and members of the opposite political party do? Or is it something more? Why does it seem to be so universal? Are there fundamentals of stupidity that can be recognized? These are the questions discussed in this book. It presents six fundamentals of stupidity that lead to the stupid choices that we see all around us. Included among these are the belief that there are no moral values, that God does not exist, and that it is acceptable to become addicted and to treat others badly and be proud. In the end we see that the only sure way to avoid the fundamentals of stupidity is through the saving power of Jesus Christ.

Adult Fiction

Miss Lydia Fairbanks and the Losers Club. Miss Lydia Fairbanks is the newest teacher at Inner City Junior High School, the deadliest school in the state. While the school principal believes she won't last a day, Miss Fairbanks quickly surprises everyone by not only surviving in the midst of her killer students, but actually thriving in the classroom. But even someone as weak and small as Miss Fairbanks can harbor secrets from the past ...

Crazy Pete. On a dark night in a lonely park in LA, crazy old Pete saves a teenager named Kelly from a suicidal encounter with a street gang. While Kelly initially resists Pete's kindness, he is gradually drawn into the life and service of his unusual mentor--a lifestyle of total concentration on others, and forgetting of himself. But even Crazy Pete has secrets, and one day, with a shock, the boy learns the terrible history of Pete's past that turned him into the saint he has become.

The Gay Illusion. Come with John as he learns that he never was gay as he had thought, nor indeed ever could be, and that gayness is a destructive illusion. (This book does not describe gay acts or contain any sexual content)

Running for the Guv. Blake Guv is a starving young attorney fresh out of law school, desperately trying to get new clients. In a mad gamble to obtain some publicity he foolishly enters the race for Governor of his state as an independent candidate. But when a series of unexpected events shove him to the front of the race, Blake is appalled at the prospect he just might win--since he hates politics with a passion!

Santa v Afton. Shortly before Christmas the tiny town of Afton is shocked when everyone is sued by a man claiming to be Santa Claus. His lawsuit is for wrongfully 'firing' him from his delivery job, since he can only come to people who believe. With less than two weeks until Christmas, will Santa's lawsuit convince them to change their minds?

Juvenile Fiction

My Science Teacher is a Wizard. Fifth grader Blake Drywater has a new wizard science teacher, who promptly turns Blake's class into roaches and earthworms. But Blake soon learns there is more than science going on in his classroom. An evil wizard is seeking a powerful potion his teacher has made. And when Blake is given the potion soon thereafter, he finds himself facing problems far harder than any science exam! Book 1 of 'The Stewards of Light' series.

My Math Teacher is a Vampire. Blake Drywater and his fellow unfortunate students at Millard Fillmore Middle School once more find themselves facing an unexpected creature in one of their classes. Because of a sudden 'neck disorder' suffered by their math teacher, Blake and his classmates receive a chilling substitute. His name is Mr. Coagulate, who has a strange fascination with blood and dreams. Book 2 of 'The Stewards of Light' series.

My History Teacher is a Leprechaun. Blake Drywater has a new history teacher--a leprechaun who escorts Blake to the underground time tunnels of his people. These tunnels are full of doors that open to different places and times, including the future. But then Blake discovers the real reason for his visit, and how it just might destroy the world!

Detectives in Diapers: They Mystery of the Aztec Amulet. Flo and Mo are not ordinary babies. Although they are only fourteen months old, they can use a computer, trick any mindless adult they want, and help their goofy detective father solve baffling crimes. Then a mysterious girl comes to their father, claiming that her grandmother has disappeared. Will the babies' superior brains be able to solve the mystery and save their bumbling parents?

<u>Cloud Trouble</u>. Inventor Uncle Ned has discovered that clouds are alive and can be transformed into common objects. He gives his nephew Talmage a cloud turned into a pen, with the assignment to see what it says and does. However, Talmage soon learns that THIS cloud is nothing but trouble since it insults everyone they meet! And since no one believes pens can talk, they think Talmage is the one saying the insults!

ABOUT THE AUTHOR

Duane L. Ostler was raised in Southern Idaho, where the wind never stops. He has lived in Australia, Mexico, Brazil, China, the big Island of Hawaii, and—most foreign of all—New Jersey. He has driven an ice cream truck, sold auto parts, been a tax collector, and sued people as an attorney. He has also obtained a PhD in law. He and his wife have five children and two cats. If you would like to contact Mr. Ostler you can reach him at: duanelostler@gmail.com

www.ingramcontent.com/pod-product-compliance
Lightning Source LLC
Chambersburg PA
CBHW072044280526
45788CB00006B/2180